VIOLENT CRIMES
AND OTHER FORMS OF
VICTIMIZATION
IN RESIDENCE HALLS

By Carolyn J. Palmer

The Higher Education Administration Series
Edited by Donald D. Gehring and D. Parker Young

COLLEGE ADMINISTRATION PUBLICATIONS, INC.

College Administration Publications, Inc.,
P. O. Box 15898, Asheville, NC 28813-0898

©1993 College Administration Publications, Inc.,
All rights reserved. Published 1993
Printed in the United States of America

Library of Congress Cataloging-in-Publication Data

Palmer, Carolyn J.
   Violent crimes and other forms of victimization in residence halls
/   by Carolyn J. Palmer.
     p.   cm. — (The Higher education administration series)
   Includes bibliographical references.
   ISBN 0-912557-15-X : $14.95
   1. College students—United States—Crimes against. 2. Student
housing—United States. 3. Violent crimes—United States.
I. Series.
HV6250.4.S78P35   1993
378.1'88—dc20   93-18795
                                                                                                                                 CIP

Brief quotation may be used in critical articles or reviews. For any other reproduction of the book, however, including electronic, mechanical, photocopying, recording or other means, written permission must be obtained from the publisher.

The views expressed in this book are those of the individual authors and are not necessarily those of College Administration Publications, Inc.

This publication is designed to provide accurate and authoritative information in regard to the subject matter covered. It is sold with the understanding that the publisher is not engaged in rendering legal, accounting or other professional service. If legal advice or other expert assistance is required, the services of a competent professional person should be sought.

                —*from a Declaration of Principles jointly adopted by a committee*
                   of the American Bar Association and a committee of publishers.

Table of Contents

Foreword · *vii*

Preface · *xi*

Acknowledgments · *xv*

About the Author · *xvii*

I. Violence and Other Forms of Victimization in Society and on Campus · 1
    Society and Its Effects on College Students · 1
    Violence and Victimization on Campus · 2
        Headline News · 3
        Incidents Not Reported by the News Media · 3
    Why the Incidence of Victimization Is Not Accurately Reflected in Research Reports and Crime Statistics · 4
        Some Incidents Are Not Crimes or Evidence of Crimes Is Lacking · 4
        Victims and Witnesses Do Not Report Incidents · 4
        Front-Line Staff Do Not Report Incidents · 5
        Institutional Officials Do Not Report Incidents · 5
    The Myth of the Campus as a Sanctuary · 6
    How Pervasive is Campus Violence? · 6
    Why Is Campus Violence a Common Topic for Study Today? · 7
        Human Rights Movements · 7
        Institutional Responsibilities or Duties Defined by Law · 8
    Summary · 9

II. Introduction to a Study of Victimization in Residence Halls • 11
Purposes of the Study • 11
The Survey Form and Other Materials • 12
Description of Participating Institutions • 14
Summary • 17

III. Institutional Characteristics • 19
Institutional Values • 19
Staff Training and Student Programming Regarding Diversity Issues • 20
Attitudes and Behaviors of Students • 21
Institutional Policies • 22
A Brief Summary of Additional Findings • 22

IV. Incidents of Violence and Victimization in Residence Halls • 25
Incidents That Were Officially Reported • 25
Estimates of Incidents Believed to Have Occurred • 26
Identifying Offenders and Adjudicating Incidents • 27

V. Descriptions of the "Most Common" and "Most Serious" Incidents • 31
Victimization of Resident Assistants (RAs) • 31
  Most Common Incidents • 31
  Most Serious Incidents • 33
Victimization of Women • 35
  Most Common Incidents • 35
  Most Serious Incidents • 37
Victimization of Racial/Ethnic Minority Students • 39
  Most Common Incidents • 39
  Most Serious Incidents • 41
Victimization of Gay/Lesbian Students • 43
  Most Common Incidents • 43
  Most Serious Incidents • 44
Victimization of Jewish Students • 46
  Most Common Incidents • 46
  Most Serious Incidents • 47
Summary • 48

VI. Suggestions and Issues Identified by Housing Officers • 51
Institutional and Personal Values • 51

Policies • 52
    Harassment Policies • 53
    Staff Policies • 54
    Alcohol and Weapons Policies • 57
Staff Training • 57
Student Programming • 60
Confronting and Reporting Incidents • 63
Adjudicating Incidents • 63
Victim Services • 64
Additional Suggestions • 65
Additional Professional Issues • 65

VII. Institutional Responses to Victimization • 67
No Single Model Will Suffice • 67
Primary, Secondary, and Tertiary Responses • 67
Recognizing the Problem and Factors
  Associated With It • 68
Putting Violence and Intolerance
  on Our Priority List • 69
Involving Institutional Leaders • 69
Environmental Assessment
  and Long-Term Planning • 71
Educating Students and Staff • 71
    Recognize That One Program
      Is Never Enough • 71
    Maximize the Use of "Teachable Moments" • 72
    Never Underestimate the Power
      of the Peer Group • 72
Exercising Our Own First Amendment Rights • 73
Understanding the Consequences of Victimization • 74
Providing Services to Victims and Offenders • 76
Building Bridges Between the Institution's Disciplinary
  System and Society's Criminal Justice System • 77
Summary • 78

VIII. Recommended Resources • 81

References • 89

Appendix A • 93
Cover Letter • 93

Appendix B • 95
Survey • 95

Violence, Vandalism, and Verbal Harassment:
  A Study of Victimization in Residence Halls • 95
Information Concerning Your Campus
  and Residence Hall System • 97
Victim Group 1: Resident Assistants (RAs) • 100
Victim Group 2: Racial/Ethnic Minority Students • 102
Victim Group 3: Women Students • 104
Victim Group 4: Gay/Lesbian Students • 106
Victim Group 5: Jewish Students • 108

Tables
1. Description of Participating Institutions • 15
2. Characteristics of Residents, RAs, and RDs • 16
3. Institutional Values • 19
4. Staff Training and Student Programming • 21
5. Student Attitudes and Behaviors • 22
6. Numbers of Incidents Actually Reported • 25
7. Reported Incidents as Percentages of
   Total Incidents Believed to Have Occurred • 26
8. Outcomes of Reported Incidents • 28
9. Outcomes of Reported Incidents
   (Five Victim Groups) • 29

Foreword

Reading the headlines of any local newspaper makes each of us aware that crime and violence in our society is growing at an alarming rate. The reasons for this dramatic increase have been, and will be, discussed by historians, educators, law makers and law enforcement personnel for many years. As many professional administrators in higher education know, today's campuses are reflections of our society. For someone to be surprised that campus crime and violence is increasing at a dramatic rate, would indicate that they are not necessarily in touch with what is happening on most of our campuses.

Campus violence became a byword for most media personalities in the early 1990s quoting the number of rapes, robberies, and aggravated assaults that were occurring on the campuses. Campus crime became so prevalent that the Congress of the United States enacted the Student Right To Know and Campus Security Act of 1990. This act requires university personnel to report campus incidents of murder, robbery, sexual offenses, aggravated assault, burglary, and motor vehicle thefts as well as arrests relating to liquor, drug, and weapon laws violations. A comparison of the number of institutions reporting campus crimes voluntarily to the FBI and those reporting campus crimes as a requirement of the Campus Security Act of 1990 is startling. In 1991, 437 institutions reported their campus crimes to the FBI. Those institutions voluntarily reported a total of 8 murders, 387 rapes, 735 armed robberies, 2,127 aggravated assaults, 14,934 burglaries, 111,783 larcenies-thefts, 4,294 motor vehicle thefts and 624 cases of arson.

In a summary article by Douglas Liederman (1993) in the *Chronicle of Higher Education*, 2,350 post-secondary institutions reported their campus crime statistics for 1991 under the Campus Security Act of 1990. Liederman's summary chart noted 30 murders, 993 rapes, 1,822 robberies, 4,669 aggravated assaults, 32,127 burglaries, and 8,981 motor vehicle thefts. The number of arrests for violation of liquor laws was 19,613, drug laws 2,920, and weapons laws 1,566. It becomes obvious why Congress now requires institutions to report criminal activity. The difference between 437 institutions' voluntary reporting and 2,350 institutions reporting because they are required to, is remarkable.

It appears to me that the inaction of higher education has brought about a congressional reaction that does not shed much positive light on our administration. Not that institutions are responsible for the crime that occurs, but in the fact that we have not honestly informed our students, faculty, staff, and general public on the level of crime on our campus.

The research completed by Dr. Carolyn J. Palmer clearly demonstrates the need for administrators, particularly those in higher level positions, to listen to residence hall staff members who, in many situations are working with life-threatening situations. As the ACUHO-I Foundation worked with Dr. Palmer in the development of this project, it became evident that she opened secret doors and ruffled some feathers within our own profession as well as other administrative positions in higher education. However, this information has been suppressed long enough. A letter Carolyn sent to the ACUHO-I Foundation, in June, 1992, really directs attention to the problem of developing a solid solution. She stated:

> I lost track of how many respondents said a major issue is getting others to take every incident seriously. I think it all comes down to institutional values (i.e., that certain things won't be tolerated in the academic community) and how we communicate these values in all we do—via public statements by institutional leaders, in our admissions and hiring practices, in our policies and programs, in the way we handle disciplinary incidents, etc. There are, of course, institutional leaders who are willing to "stand up and be heard" or otherwise speak out on diversity or harassment issues. But some of them are apparently not willing to "put their money where their mouths are" in supporting the types of staff/faculty development programs, educational/academic programs for students, etc. that seem to be desperately needed.

In developing her research, Dr. Palmer identified four study groups and then later included a fifth group, the RA staff, at ACUHO-I's request since some preliminary work had already been completed by Schuh and Shipton, (1993), relating to violent acts toward residence hall staff. The five groups were: (a) racial and ethnic minority students, (b) gay and lesbian students, (c) Jewish students, (d) women students (e) resident assistants (RAs). With the identified groups, Dr. Palmer assessed the scope and nature of incidents of violence, vandalism, and verbal harassment as they affect these groups in selected samples of housing operations. Following an extensive review of the literature and an outline of her methodology, Dr. Palmer disclosed a survey return rate of 49 institutions or approximately a 39 percent rate. The

49 institutions responding are located in 30 different states and house approximately 141,000 students. Further demographics are provided throughout this study to give the housing professional a basis for institutional comparison. One of the more unusual aspects of Dr. Palmer's research is the report of incidents that the participating institutions "believed" to have occurred against the five groups.

Though the information is provided as professional judgments, as Dr. Palmer notes, "we must assume that the individual responding is well informed of what actually occurs in the halls whether the information is officially recorded or not." Dr. Palmer provided considerable space for individual comments from the five groups. The compilation of individual circumstances helps establish the critical nature of many of these situations.

The final portion of this book deals with potential directions housing professionals might follow in developing solutions. However, these solutions cannot be developed for the campus alone; the development process must include the entire community. Because students come from a variety of cultural backgrounds, they will as noted earlier, reflect the values and standards of their origins. The problem is not what campus personnel can do; the problem is what the entire community can do. The campus administration might well be the initiator, but total community involvement is essential.

I sincerely hope that you will review this study closely. The results of this research is important to our colleagues, and to the decision-makers at the highest level of our institutions. The problems have been defined. The solutions are difficult to determine. For these reasons, a joint effort by faculty, staff, students, government officials, law enforcement, and the general public is required.

> —James C. Grimm, Director of Housing, University of Florida; Chair, ACUHO-I Foundation, Board of Trustees

Preface

Concerns about violence and other forms of victimization are increasing throughout our society. Even on college campuses, once thought to provide "sanctuary" from the problems of the "real world," incidents of violence, vandalism, and verbal harassment are occurring at an alarming rate.

Members of historically disenfranchised groups (e.g., racial/ethnic minority students, women students, Jewish students, and gay/lesbian students) are often victimized by those who engage in hate-speech or other forms of verbal abuse, activities that damage or destroy personal or public property, and acts of violence that are often associated with racism, sexism, anti-Semitism, and homophobia. The physical, social, emotional, and educational consequences of victimization are great. Indeed, some students withdraw from higher education entirely after experiencing campus environments perceived as inhospitable, hostile, or dangerous.

Most college and university housing professionals realize that many and perhaps most of the incidents of victimization occurring on their campuses occur in their residence halls, primarily because this is where most students on a residential campus are at night, on weekends, and (in many cases) after they have consumed alcohol. Since the front-line, live-in staff known as resident assistants (RAs) are the institutional employees most likely called upon to deal with disruptive students at such times, they too are often the victims of violence, vandalism, and verbal harassment.

A large portion of this book summarizes the results of a national study of victimization in residence halls. Chief housing officers at selected institutions completed a survey concerning incidents affecting members of five victim groups: RAs and racial/ethnic minority, Jewish, gay/lesbian, and women students. Although it is presumed that the primary readers will be housing professionals, the results of the study itself indicate that college officials in administrative units other than housing would also benefit from informing themselves of the many issues addressed in this book. In fact, it is suggested that major problems resulting in the victimization of students and staff in residence halls cannot be solved without the direct involvement and assistance of institutional leaders at the very top of the organizational hierarchy.

This book has been written for practitioners. The terminology and writing style were chosen to enable those with no research background whatsoever to easily understand the results and implications of the research that is summarized. The chapters are intended to be read in sequential order, but some readers may wish to skip some chapters and focus on specific chapters or sections that they find most meaningful or useful.

Chapter I provides an introduction to violent crimes and other forms of victimization in society, on campus, and in residence halls. It also examines why many incidents of violence, vandalism, and verbal harassment are not reported and shows how human rights movements, legislation, and litigation have inspired recent examinations of the problems associated with victimization in higher education.

A study of victimization in residence halls (i.e., its purposes, methods, and participants) is introduced in Chapter II.

Institutional values, staff training and student programming regarding diversity issues, student attitudes and behaviors, policies, and other characteristics of respondent institutions are summarized in Chapter III.

Chapter IV focuses on *numbers* of incidents of violence, vandalism, and verbal harassment affecting each of the five groups at respondent institutions during the previous two years. These include numbers of incidents that respondents believe actually occurred; that were "officially reported"; that had offenders identified; that led to disciplinary hearings; that yielded disciplinary sanctions; and that resulted in sanctions that respondents believed were sufficient to deter offenders from repeating similar behaviors in the future.

Chapter V provides *descriptions* of incidents that respondents identified as the "most common" and the "most serious" ones victimizing members of each of the five victim groups in their residence halls.

Suggestions that respondents would offer to their colleagues and issues they believe should be explored in reference to preventing the occurrence of victimization, or most effectively addressing victimization if it does occur, are summarized in Chapter VI.

In Chapter VII the author reinforces and adds to many of the suggestions made by the housing officers who participated in this study in reference to how institutions of higher education should respond to issues of violence and other forms of victimization on campus.

Finally, Chapter VIII provides brief annotations of various resources recommended for readers who wish to learn more about campus violence, the victimization of staff, racial harassment, diversity programs, legal issues, and other topics addressed in this book.

It is emphasized throughout this book that there is no single approach to addressing problems of violent crimes and other forms of victimization that will "fit" all institutions. It is recommended that readers use the information contained in this book to inspire discussions on their own campuses, assess and examine their own problems, and develop institution-specific strategies for solving those problems. Knowing that one is not alone in facing many problems in today's residence halls can be very supportive, but the problems cannot be solved until housing officers and others take appropriate action on their own campuses.

Acknowledgments

The project summarized in this book was funded by a research grant provided by the Research and Educational Foundation of the Association of College and University Housing Officers-International (ACUHO-I) and a basic grant provided by the Faculty Research Committee of Bowling Green State University. I am very grateful to both organizations for their support of research concerning what I believe are critical issues facing higher education in the United States today.

I wish to express my sincere gratitude to all of the housing officers at selected ACUHO-I member institutions who participated in the study and to Jim Grimm, Mike Hoctor, Garry Johnson, Gary Schwarzmueller, and other ACUHO-I leaders who provided information, feedback, and moral support as the study progressed.

The major findings from this study formed the foundation for an ACUHO College and an ACUHO-I conference session during the summer of 1992. The information and perspectives shared by workshop participants and co-presenters, Helen Ellison, Leontye Lewis, Eleanor Reynolds, and Bill Schnackel, have been extremely valuable in preparing the final manuscript for this book.

In addition, I wish to thank Don Gehring for reviewing the drafts of my manuscript and offering many helpful suggestions for improvement. A special note of gratitude is expressed to Leontye Lewis, who served as the graduate assistant for the research project summarized in this book, not only for her fine work in completing many project tasks, but also for her genuine concern for residence hall students and staff and her insights regarding the problems addressed in the study.

— Carolyn J. Palmer

About the Author

Carolyn J. Palmer is currently an assistant professor in the Department of Higher Education and Student Affairs at Bowling Green State University and has served as a resident director and Assistant Director of Housing at the University of Illinois.

Dr. Palmer received her bachelor's degree (magna cum laude) in human development from the University of Massachusetts, her master's degree in counseling from the University of Connecticut, and her Ph.D. in quantitative and evaluative research methodologies from the University of Illinois, where she received the College of Education Alumni Association's award for the most outstanding doctoral graduate of 1987.

Dr. Palmer is also the recipient of the Outstanding Research Award from Commission III (Residence Halls) of the American College Personnel Association and both the Professional Development Award and Distinguished Service Award from the Great Lakes Association of College and University Housing Officers. She has published several articles and presented many conference sessions on topics related to victimization in residence halls, rape and other violence against women on campus, hate speech, alcohol, and other issues addressed in this book.

Chapter I

Violence and Other Forms of Victimization in Society and on Campus

SOCIETY AND ITS EFFECTS ON COLLEGE STUDENTS

Ours is an increasingly violent society. A recent report from the Federal Bureau of Investigation indicated that "violent crimes by people of all ages reached a record high last year ... up 4% from 1990 and 33% since 1982" (FBI, 1992, p. 1). Perpetrators and victims of violent crime include persons of both genders and all ages, races, religions, social classes, educational levels, and lifestyles living in all types of communities. In fact, FBI statistics showed that the 1990-1991 increase in crime was "3% in cities, 4% in suburbs, 5% in rural areas" (FBI, 1992, p. 1).

It has become almost impossible to open a newspaper or turn on a radio or television set without being reminded of the incidence of violent crime in our own neighborhoods. Along with violence, the daily news often includes accounts of vandalism and verbal harassment based on race, ethnicity, religion, sexual orientation, gender and any number of other personal characteristics. As a result, terms such as "hate crimes," "acts of intolerance," "hate speech," and "harassment" have become parts of our working vocabulary.

College students, along with all other people, are products of the society in which they have spent their lives, and institutions of higher education are integral parts of that society. Consequently, college campuses are not immune from the types of violent crimes and other forms of victimization that currently plague our country. Although this book focuses on the college campus in general and the residence hall environment in particular, one should not conclude that incidents of violence, vandalism, and verbal harassment occurring on the college campus are, in either frequency or severity, equal to or greater than such incidents occurring in many American communities today.

In order to resist the temptation to "blame" college officials, young people in general, or college students in particular for the problems addressed in this book, please consider this question: how reasonable is it to expect that 18-year-olds can step onto a college campus or move into a residence hall and resolve overnight all of the social problems that all of our society's adults, with all of their wisdom, throughout all of our history, have not been able to solve?

Because community housing patterns throughout much of the United States are related to race, ethnicity, socio-economic status, etc., most people live in rather homogeneous neighborhoods. As a result, many students enter college with little or no previous experience with cultural diversity. Students who choose to live off-campus often live in fraternity or sorority houses, apartments, or houses with people who are much like themselves. And graduates often move to homogeneous neighborhoods resembling those of their childhood. Thus, it appears reasonable to suggest that the college or university residence hall, where people of many races, religions, national origins, lifestyles, value systems, etc. live together, may be the most culturally diverse environment in which many of today's college students will *ever* live.

The transition to a heterogeneous living environment is difficult for many students, particularly those who have been taught to ignore, avoid, suspect, resent, fear, or even hate people who are different from themselves. Whenever large numbers of people live together, misunderstandings and conflicts are inevitable. However, it appears that some students have considerably more difficulty than others in solving interpersonal problems in constructive ways.

Helping students learn to communicate, to compromise, and to resolve and even respect their differences so that they can live together in harmony, with civility, and with true appreciation for having the opportunity to know and learn from each other, is a challenge facing today's housing professionals. Indeed, the development of respect and appreciation for ideological, cultural, lifestyle and other "differences" is highly valued within the academic community. Consequently, many administrators, faculty, staff, and students work continuously to help increasingly diverse populations on our nation's campuses to develop relationships and perspectives that will contribute to their effectiveness as participants in and leaders of our increasingly pluralistic society.

VIOLENCE AND VICTIMIZATION ON CAMPUS

During recent years, access to higher education has been provided to increased numbers of racial, ethnic, and other minority group members. However, it appears that bringing such students onto a campus and placing them in residence halls, classrooms, and other facilities or programs with majority students may not be sufficient to ensure their effective incorporation within the social or academic communities of the institution, their access to truly equal educational opportunities, their satisfaction with the college experience, or their retention and achievement in college (Astin, 1982; Fleming, 1984; Sedlacek, 1987; Taylor, 1986).

As student populations become more diverse, students sharing common characteristics are becoming more vocal in requesting or demanding that their specific needs or problems be addressed. Some groups of students whose presence was once tolerated or simply ignored by other students may be approaching "critical mass" levels, in the sense that their increased numbers, visibility, or activity on campus may be perceived as discomforting or upsetting to those not associated with the groups in question. Tragically, some students have responded to those who are different from themselves with violence, vandalism, or verbal harassment (Marable, 1988).

Headline News

Recent news reports of racial, anti-Semitic, homophobic, sexual, and all other forms of violence and harassment on campus are very disturbing not only to administrators and faculty, but also to students, parents, and other constituencies. Please consider the following headlines taken from *The Chronicle of Higher Education* or institution-specific newspapers during the past two years:

- Anti-Semitic Incidents up Sharply on Campuses
- Campus Hebrew House Defiled by Vandals
- 3 Arrested in Assault on Jewish Students
- 2 Student Papers Denounced for Anti-Semitic Remarks
- Vandals Paint Racial Slurs on Rutgers Jewish Center
- Yale Students Organize Boycott to Protest Racism
- Asians at U. of Minnesota Receive Racist Letter
- 2 Fraternities Suspended After Racial Incidents
- Assailants Beat Student They Thought Was Arab
- President Apologizes for Racial Comments
- Affirmative-Action Officer Accused of Ethnic Slurs
- Offensive Cartoon Sparks Incidents in Dormitory
- Dormitory Floor Closed After Harassment
- Homosexual-Rights Advocates at Yale Ask President to Denounce Bias
- Increase in Reports of Sexual Assaults Strains Campus Disciplinary Systems
- 9 CSU Students Indicted: 7 Athletes, 2 Others Accused of Rape in Dormitory
- 4 Women Sue Carleton College For Not Protecting Them From Sexual Assault
- Gunshots Strike Women's Dorm at UT
- College Bans Parties After Stabbings
- U. of Iowa Mourns Shooting Victims

Incidents Not Reported by the News Media

Similarly disturbing are the many incidents that are not considered "serious enough" to come to the attention of or to be reported by the news media, but that create difficult, unequal, intimidating, or hostile living and learning environments in which many students must function on our campuses.

> For racial and other minorities, insensitivity or outright hostility on the part of other students may seriously disrupt academic work. Cases of verbal and even physical violence against racial and other minorities, widely reported in the press, represent a deplorable extreme, but less dramatic forms of antagonism can still interfere with learning. (United States Department of Education, 1990, p. 6)

Although many incidents of verbal harassment, vandalism, or violence may not be deemed "newsworthy," they often have an adverse impact on students at many types and sizes of institutions in many different locations across the country.

WHY THE INCIDENCE OF VICTIMIZATION IS NOT ACCURATELY REFLECTED IN RESEARCH REPORTS AND CRIME STATISTICS

Incidents of victimization that actually occur may far outnumber not only those reported by the press, but those examined in our research, those discussed in our professional publications, and those summarized in official crime statistics. For example, Sherrill (1989) reported that, "other than a flurry of books and articles that have dealt specifically with student civil unrest of the late sixties and early seventies, the scope of literature on campus violence has been less than imposing" (pp. 89-90).

A common explanation for the scarcity of research concerning violence on campus is that reliable data are difficult to obtain, in part because such data are missing or lost at each step of the reporting process, from the victim or witness level to the institutional or national level.

Some Incidents Are Not Crimes or Evidence of Crimes Is Lacking

Of course, many campus crimes are reported by law enforcement personnel and subsequently appear in national statistics. However, many incidents of concern may not be included in crime statistics, primarily because they are not reported to campus police. In some cases (e.g., some verbal statements perceived as offensive to others, but representing expression protected by the First Amendment), no actual crimes are involved. In other cases, particularly when victims or witnesses do not provide complete and timely information, it may be difficult to determine whether crimes were indeed committed.

Victims and Witnesses Do Not Report Incidents

The psychological responses to violence, particularly in the initial stage of victimization, are often associated with feelings of shock, fear, confusion, helplessness, and numbness (Cerio, 1989). Consequently, the very process of victimization itself may render many victims unable or unwilling to report the incident to police, campus staff, or others. Unfortunately, many persons who witness a violent or other harmful or offensive event may also experience emotional turmoil associated with repression or avoidance leading to "I didn't see or hear anything," "it's none of my business," or "I don't want to get involved."

In many cases, neither victims nor witnesses ever bring the incident to the attention of staff. As a result, perhaps the greatest numbers of incidents not reported *by* institutional officials are those not reported *to* those officials.

Front-Line Staff Do Not Report Incidents

Another concern is that incidents coming to the attention of some staff may not be reported further, as those staff believe the behavior is not serious enough to report, believe that the problem has been resolved at their level, do not wish to embarrass or punish the students involved, realize that victims and witnesses are unwilling to testify, or believe there is nothing that police or disciplinary officers can or will do to rectify the situation.

Common Behaviors Are Identified as Normative Behaviors

Sherrill and Siegel (1989) stated that "a college community, particularly one that is largely residential, might become inured to a certain amount of violence and thus allow it to go unreported" (p. 1). It is conceivable that some forms of violence, vandalism, or verbal abuse in residence halls have become so commonplace that they are considered to be within the range of normative behaviors or behaviors to be expected on the part of a certain percentage of the student population and therefore are not officially reported.

Victimization of Staff is Accepted as Part of the Job

Durant, Marston, and Eisenhandler (1986) conducted a survey of almost 6,000 resident advisers at 284 institutions and found that, while 84 percent of these residence hall staff members had been the victims of harassment (e.g., offensive language, pranks, graffiti, or harassing phone calls), only ten percent had officially reported the incidents. Instead, many chose to settle the matter with the offenders directly, discuss the incident informally with peers or others, or simply ignore the abuse.

Rickgarn (1989) noted that "RAs tend to shrug off actions against them as 'coming with the territory'" (p. 31). Perhaps this may help to explain the findings from a study of resident assistants on one campus reported by Schuh and Shipton (1983). Their study involved the abuse of staff and included racial slurs directed to minority staff and sexual slurs directed to female staff. Of the 64 incidents reported in the study, only two, both of them involving physical violence, had been formally reported for institutional judicial action.

Institutional Officials Do Not Report Incidents

Although it seems clear that many incidents of victimization on college campuses are not reported by victims, witnesses, or "front-line" staff to institutional officials, it is also possible that some institutional officials who do receive reports of such victimization may not wish to communicate that information further. For example, Rickgarn (1989) suggested that the difficulties in obtaining pertinent information from institutions of higher education may account for the scarcity of literature on the topic of violence in residence halls between 1934 and very recent years:

> But clearly violence in residence halls is not new. While it may be ignored or denied, violence has existed since the beginning of residential units on the campuses of this country. Cowley (1934), in his history of student housing, discussed various incidents of violence that were directed against residence hall staff. Campus violence, however, was not a popular topic then (any more than it is now), as administrators did not want reports of misconduct to damage the reputations of their institutions or to create negative impressions among prospective students and parents. So, for many years after Cowley's work, little was written about violence on campus. Part of this may have been due to protectionism and the lack of acknowledgment of various forms of violence against women and minorities that characterized a lengthy period of our history. But it is more likely that the issues were either ignored or denied to avoid any potential embarrassment to the institution. (pp. 29-30)

THE MYTH OF THE CAMPUS AS A SANCTUARY

Regardless of the not uncommon perception of a college campus as an environment that provides sanctuary from the harsh realities of the outside world, violence, vandalism, and verbal abuse are not new problems within higher education. "In fact, campuses have never been without crime and violence, although the nature and extent of the campus crime seen today clearly have never existed before" (Smith, 1989a, p. 5).

Similarly, "violence in residence halls is neither unknown nor uncommon; rather, it appears to be far more pervasive than most administrators or students would care to admit" (Rickgarn, 1989, p. 39).

> Violence on college campuses is not only, as was once thought, imported by nonstudents. Results from the Towson State University Campus Violence Surveys indicate that most violence on college campuses is student-to-student violence and that only a portion of the violence that actually occurs is reported. Yet the myth of the safe campus endures. The FBI's *Uniform Crime Report,* to which 10 to 15 percent of campuses subscribe, does not begin to tell the whole story. (Sherrill & Siegel, 1989, p. 1)

HOW PERVASIVE IS CAMPUS VIOLENCE?

In 1987, the *Uniform Crime Report,* issued by the Federal Bureau of Investigation (FBI), indicated that there were several thousand crimes of violence toward persons and more than 100,000 crimes involving property reported on campuses annually (United States Department of Justice, 1987; cited in Smith, 1989a). However, Smith (1989a) emphasized that these figures underestimated the actual totals, because fewer than one-fifth of the nation's colleges and universities reported their crime statistics to the FBI at that time. In addition, Smith stated that, "because institutions want to project positive public images, there is reason to suspect that some colleges' reports are understated" (p. 9).

Estimates of the prevalence of violence on college campuses have been found to vary according to the roles of persons issuing such estimates. For example, a study conducted in 1985 found the following:

> Many more students said they had either been victims of some form of violence or knew of a greater number of violent incidents than our official reports indicated. It also became apparent that some of our own offices on campus—the Residence Department, for example—had a different perception of the amount of violence that occurred on campus than did other offices such as the campus police. (Cockey, Sherrill, & Cave, 1989, p. 18)

Incidents of victimization on campus are perhaps most likely to occur at night or on weekends, when resident students are not in classes, but in or near campus housing units. Although residence hall staff represent only one group of staff on duty at such times, it is conceivable that their live-in status enables them to become aware of more subtle, behind-the-scenes, minor, and perhaps even major incidents than come to the attention of campus police or other officials.

WHY IS CAMPUS VIOLENCE A COMMON TOPIC FOR STUDY TODAY?

Perhaps the two most significant factors inspiring research on campus violence, after a considerable period of relative silence on this topic, are various types of human rights movements and recent legislation and litigation involving the responsibilities or duties of administrators and other persons employed by institutions of higher education.

Human Rights Movements

Sherrill (1989) indicated that the feminist movement has contributed to the study of violence against women. Such study has found that "women have been and continue to be direct victims of such violent acts as stranger rape, date rape, sexual harassment, and courtship violence" (Cerio, 1989, p. 54). Rickgarn (1989) suggested that the most underreported form of violence that occurs in residence halls may be acquaintance rape. It appears that courtship violence may be grossly underreported. Bogal-Allbritten and Allbritten (1985) surveyed residence hall students and found that 19% of the respondents had experienced and 61% of the respondents knew of another student who had experienced some form of courtship violence.

Just as the movement concerning women's rights has encouraged the study of the victimization of women, other human rights movements have encouraged the study of the victimization of racial/ethnic minorities and Jewish, gay/lesbian/bisexual, and other sub-groups of students.

> Violence done to members of those groups that have historically been disenfranchised—such as gays and racial and ethnic minorities—continues to be unreported. The AIDS epidemic has given a new intensity to violent homophobia, and unfortunately, anti-Semitism and racism live on college campuses just as they do in most American communities. Vandalism seems to occur with greater frequency than in the past. Anonymous graffiti have given way to major property destruction ... (Sherrill & Siegel, 1989, p. 1)

The issue of human rights may be of particular concern to many today because of recent public attention given to what have come to be known as "hate crimes."

> Violent acts against minority and ethnic groups have increased over the past several years ... The incidents range from racial slurs and taunting to beatings ... Gay men and lesbian women on college campuses—both students and faculty—are victims of violence inspired by homophobia. As reported in "In Brief" (1987a), a Holocaust memorial at the University of Denver was vandalized four times within the week that the memorial was erected. As reported in "In Brief" (1987b), homosexuals encounter abuse such as death threats and harassing phone calls and letters ... (Cerio, 1989, p. 54)

Institutional Responsibilities or Duties Defined by Law

Another factor contributing to the recent attention given to this topic involves the changing nature of institutional responsibilities or duties as defined by law. Barr (1989) noted that much of the rapidly increasing amount of litigation involving institutions of higher education has been based on claims of liability due to negligence. "There are three legal elements in a negligence claim: duty, breach of that duty, and the breach being the proximate cause of the injury" (Barr, 1989, p. 97).

Smith (1989a) discussed several legal duties for institutions of higher education as they may pertain to campus violence. Perhaps two of the duties of greatest concern to housing professionals, particularly given their landlord-tenant special and contractual relationship with resident students, are the duty to provide adequate protective or safety measures (e.g., locking mechanisms, lighting systems, security guards, etc.) and the duty to warn potential victims of any dangers. Schuh (1988) emphasized the duty to protect the safety of students in residence halls (e.g., via routine inspections of facilities and equipment) and noted the following:

> If the campus is located in a high crime area, or there is concern that students' physical safety may be threatened, resident students should be informed of ways to minimize such risks as soon as they move into the residence hall. If a series of criminal acts occur on the campus or in the residence halls and the institution fails to take

steps to rectify the situation or notify the students, the institution, through its administrators, could be held liable. (p. 251)

SUMMARY

Incidents of violence and other forms of victimization that occur on today's college campuses are generally reflective of and undoubtedly related to similar incidents that are occurring in our larger society. Reliable information regarding campus violence and other incidents perceived as being potentially embarrassing to an institution has, for many reasons, been difficult to obtain until very recent years. However, legislation, litigation, and human rights movements have emphasized that administrators have legal duties and moral obligations to provide for the safety and security of students and to warn students of potential dangers.

As a result, crimes and other incidents that victimize students are now becoming part of the public domain. Some administrators may remain reluctant to acknowledge the presence or the full extent of crime on their campuses. "Recent court decisions, however, clearly delineate the path of risk down which administrators may lead their institutions should they attempt to hide the problem" (Sherrill, 1989, p. 89).

Chapter II

Introduction to a Study of Victimization in Residence Halls

The project entitled "Violence, Vandalism, and Verbal Harassment: A Study of Victimization in Residence Halls" was supported by grants from the Research and Educational Foundation of the Association of College and University Housing Officers–International (ACUHO–I) and the Faculty Research Committee of Bowling Green State University.

College and university housing officers associated with ACUHO-I and its Research and Educational Foundation should be commended for their courage to sponsor a study concerning incidents of victimization in residence halls. These professionals apparently understand the measurement principle that "you can't cure a fever by throwing away the thermometer." That is, they realize that major problems are not likely to suddenly disappear or magically solve themselves if we simply discount, deny, ignore, or otherwise fail to assess them. Rather, our systematic efforts to identify and describe problems and the many factors related to them have the potential to yield information that may be helpful in the problem-solving process.

PURPOSES OF THE STUDY

The major purposes of this study were to assess the scope and nature of incidents of violence, vandalism, and verbal harassment as they affect selected groups of students in residence halls and to identify what housing officers believe is needed in order to most effectively address problems of victimization in residence halls.

Although any individual student or any group of students may be victimized by violence, vandalism, or verbal harassment, four victim groups were initially identified for this study. They included racial/ethnic minority students, women students, gay/lesbian students, and Jewish students. At the request of several housing officers, a fifth victim group was added. This group includes resident assistants (RAs), student staff members who live and work in college and university residence halls.

This study represents only one small step in a much larger process. The ultimate question of concern involves how higher education can assist students of many races, nations, religions, cultures, lifestyles, etc. in learning to live, learn, and work together in harmony, with a recognition of their many similarities, and with an appreciation for their many differences. Multicultural awareness programs represent one of many educational or developmental interventions designed to solve problems associated with increased diversity in the student population. But all the answers to questions involving what works and what does not work in changing students' knowledge, beliefs, attitudes, and behaviors with respect to people who are different from themselves are not clear.

What should our response be to racist, anti-Semitic, homophobic, or sexual victimization of students? How should we determine what disciplinary sanctions or involvements on the part of our criminal justice system are appropriate? How can we protect the rights and the safety of students who are at greatest risk of being victimized? What responsibilities should we assume for the legal, medical, counseling, or other assistance needed by those who have been victimized? What legal issues are involved? What policy changes may be needed? What financial investment in staff training and student programs regarding diversity issues is warranted?

This study cannot provide the definitive answers to the above questions that would "fit" all institutions or identify the perfect solutions to problems of violence, vandalism, and verbal harassment in all residence hall systems. However, a major goal of the study was to provide information that would inspire housing professionals and other administrators to acknowledge problems, discuss issues, and develop strategies for addressing victimization that may be most effective on their own campuses.

THE SURVEY FORM AND OTHER MATERIALS

Copies of survey materials are provided in the Appendix. These include a two-page cover letter, a one-page sheet defining the terminology used in the study and confirming several institutional characteristics, and a 12-page survey form. It should be noted that, for the purposes of this study, the term "violence" was defined as affecting *human beings*, whereas "vandalism" (even if perpetrated via an act that some might consider to be violent) affected *property*, and "verbal harassment" involved spoken or written language that remained at the *verbal* level. (Please see the Appendix for complete definitions of these terms.)

The first page of the survey instrument was designed to gather information regarding several characteristics of student and staff populations. Gender, race, and nationality are generally included in student and staff records. However, percentages of students and staff who are Jewish or gay/lesbian are seldom known to housing officers. Consequently, items seeking estimates of such percentages were preceded by the following statement:

- *Note:* Responses to the next two items are acknowledged as "unknowns." Leave them blank if you wish. However, if you are willing to offer an "educated guess," it will be helpful in identifying approximate percentages estimated to identify with the groups in question.

The second page of the survey form included 32 items to be rated on seven-point scales, ranging in value from 1 = *Strongly Disagree* to 7 = *Strongly Agree*. Twelve of these items assessed perceptions of institutional values. Six items assessed exposure, sensitivity, and responsiveness to issues of diversity on the part of resident assistants (RAs) and hall directors. Two items concerned diversity programming for students; eight focused on racist, homophobic, anti-Semitic and sexist attitudes and behaviors on the part of students; and four assessed the current prevalence of, and five-year changes in, racial tension and violence towards women. Three additional "yes/no" items asked if the institution had a sexual harassment policy in effect for employees, a racial harassment policy in effect for employees, and any type of harassment or "hate speech" policy in effect for students. (Please see the Appendix for a complete listing of all items.)

Two of the ten remaining pages of the survey were devoted to each of the five victim groups studied: resident assistants (RAs), racial/ethnic minority students, women students, gay/lesbian students, and Jewish students. Six questions were asked in reference to each type of incident (violence, vandalism, and verbal harassment) affecting each group of victims. That is, with only minor modifications referencing the type of incident and group in question, essentially the same six questions were asked 15 times (3 types of incidents times 5 victim groups = 15). The six questions, in this example as they pertain specifically to violence towards RAs, were worded as follows:

1. In your professional judgment *(whether or not the incidents were officially reported)*, how many incidents in your residence halls during the past two years have involved violence towards RAs?
2. How many of these incidents were actually reported?
3. In how many of the reported incidents was the offender identified?
4. How many of the offender-identified incidents led to a disciplinary hearing?
5. How many of these disciplinary hearings led to disciplinary actions or sanctions?
6. How many of the disciplinary cases resulted in sanctions that you believe were sufficient to deter the offender from repeating similar behavior in the future?

The second page of questions devoted to each of the five victim groups included four free-response items. Again, with only minor changes in the wording to identify a specific victim group, these items were identical and were presented five times (once for each of the five victim groups). Using the RA section of the survey form as an example, please note that the four free-response items were worded as follows:

- Please describe in one or two brief sentences *the most common type of incident* that victimizes RAs in your residence hall system:
- Please describe in one or two brief sentences what you would consider to be *the most serious incident* that victimized an RA in your system during the past two years:
- What suggestions, advice, or other comments would you give to other housing officers who wish to prevent the victimization of RAs and most effectively deal with such victimization if it does occur?
- Please describe any legal, social, policy, program, staff training, or other issues you believe that we as a profession should discuss or explore (for example, at conferences, in our professional publications, or in our research endeavors) in relation to preventing the victimization of RAs and most effectively dealing with such victimization if it does occur:

Finally, respondents were encouraged to attach separate sheets of paper containing any additional comments they wished to offer with respect to the victimization of each of the five groups identified in this study.

DESCRIPTION OF PARTICIPATING INSTITUTIONS

It should be clearly stated from the outset that this is a *descriptive* study focusing on the responses of housing officers at 49 institutions of higher education in the United States. Readers are urged to use great caution in making inferences to any or all other colleges and universities.

Survey materials were mailed during November of 1991 to chief housing officers at 125 ACUHO-I member institutions within the United States. The institutions within this sample were systematically selected by computer in such a way that they represented the entire population of institutions listed in the *ACUHO-I Membership Directory* according to public/private status, two-year/four-year status, location (based on ACUHO-I regions and districts), and size of residence hall system (based on numbers of students housed).

Forty-nine (39.2%) of the survey forms were completed and returned. Participation in this study is commendable, particularly because completion of the survey form required respondents to conduct their own "in-house research" involving records maintained during the previous two years. Several respondents indicated that individual staff members or committees had been assigned the tasks of reviewing residence hall incident reports, providing some of the information needed to complete the survey form, and (as an unintended positive outcome of the study) developing summaries of problems identified as a result of their review and proposals for addressing such problems on their own campuses.

Several persons who had received survey forms contacted the researcher to explain why they could not participate in the study. The more common reasons cited included the following:
- The chief housing officer did not have permission to release or did not feel comfortable releasing the type of information requested.
- All disciplinary incidents on campus were handled by students' academic departments or colleges or by a central office. Whether records were scattered across campus or maintained in a central location, data distinguishing residence hall incidents from all other incidents on campus were not available.
- Incident reports and disciplinary records for the two-year period in question were either no longer on file or not easily accessible to housing officers.

Several characteristics of the 49 participating institutions are described in Table 1. A combined total of more than half a million students are enrolled on the 49 campuses, and 141,961 of these students

TABLE 1
Description of Participating Institutions

Description	Number	Percentage/Range
Total number of institutions	49	(located in 30 states)
Public	28	(57.1%)
Private	21	(42.9%)
4-Year	48	(98.0%)
2-Year	1	(2.0%)
ACUHO-I Eastern District	12	(24.5%)
ACUHO-I Western District	10	(20.4%)
ACUHO-I Southern District	9	(18.4%)
ACUHO-I Central District	18	(36.7%)
Fewer than 1,500 residents	17	(34.7%—"small")
1,500-3,000 residents	15	(30.6%—"medium")
More than 3,000 residents	17	(34.7%—"large")
Total students enrolled	596,104	(range: 600-38,000)
Total students housed	141,961	(range:111-13,146)
Total RAs employed	3,459	(range 6-292)
Total RDs employed	448	(range 0-39)

live in residence halls. Student enrollment at individual institutions ranges from 600 to 38,000, and residence hall occupancy ranges from slightly more than 100 to more than 13,000. Of course, numbers of staff employed in residence halls also vary widely, with the numbers of resident assistants (RAs) ranging from six to 292 and the numbers of resident directors (RDs) ranging from zero to 39.

Approximately 57% of the institutions are public and 43% are private. Residence hall systems at the public institutions house an average of 3,550 students, whereas those at private institutions house an average of 2,027. Approximately 21% of the public and 52% of the private schools operate "small" residence hall systems (fewer than 1,500 residents); 32% of the public and 29% of the private schools have "medium" sized systems (1,500-3,000 residents); and 46% of the public and 19% of the private schools have "large" systems (more than 3,000 residents).

Descriptions of other demographic characteristics are based on incomplete data, as not all respondents completed every item on the survey form. For example, two respondents did not specify the numbers of men and women living in residence halls. Information provided by the remaining 47 respondents shows that approximately 51% of their residents are women and 49% are men. Percentages of men and women residents within individual institutions range from zero to 100%, as two institutions house only women and one houses only men.

TABLE 2
Characteristics of Residents, RAs, and RDs

Characteristics	Residents	RAs	RDs
n=	46 schools 117,170 res.	48 schools 3,365 RAs	44 schools 448 RDs
White (non-Hispanic)	77.4%	77.2%	77.9%
African-American	8.9%	11.9%	13.4%
Asian-American *and* Hawaiian/Pacific Islander	6.6%	5.0%	1.8%
Hispanic/Latino	4.6%	3.9%	3.6%
Other racial/ethnic identity	1.6%	1.4%	2.7%
Alaskan Native *and* Native American Indian	.9%	.5%	.6%
n=	33 schools 76,161 res.	36 schools 2,210 RAs	38 schools 381 RDs
Jewish (Estimates)	8.1%	4.5%	5.4%
n=	34 schools 105,372 res.	35 schools 2,470 RAs	35 schools 337 RDs
Gay/Lesbian (Estimates)	9.9%	9.2%	11.3%

Approximately 94% of the residents are undergraduates and 6% are graduate students; 94% are Americans and 6% are international students. As noted in Table 2, the majority (between 77 and 78%) of the residents, resident assistants (RAs), and resident directors (RDs) are white. However, it should be noted that resident student populations vary from approximately 46% white on one campus to 97% white on another. African-Americans comprise the second largest groups of residents (9%), RAs (12%), and RDs (13%). Numbers of students and staff identifying with the smaller racial/ethnic groups vary considerably according to the location of the institution. For example, almost all of Alaskan native residents, all six of the Alaskan native RAs, and the only Alaskan native RD identified in this study are located in the state of Alaska.

Table 2 also shows that only between 33 and 38 of the 49 respondents chose to offer "educated guesses" with respect to how many of their students and staff are Jewish or gay/lesbian. Several respondents indicated that they had zero Jewish residents because their institutions are Catholic or Christian. In addition, some noted that, because of the religious affiliation of the institution or for other reasons, whatever homosexuality may exist is kept "underground" and is thus impossible to estimate.

SUMMARY

This study of victimization in residence halls focuses on incidents of violence, vandalism, and verbal harassment perpetrated against (1) resident assistants (RAs), (2) racial/ethnic minority students, (3) women students, (4) gay/lesbian students, and (5) Jewish students in residence halls at 49 ACUHO-I member institutions during the two years between 1989 and 1991. Chief housing officers at these institutions reported that their residence hall systems employ a total of 3,459 RAs and house a total of 141,961 students (approximately 51% women, 23% racial/ethnic minorities, 10% gay/lesbian students, and 8% Jewish students).

The results of this study are based on the responses of these 49 housing officers to a twelve-page survey form designed to assess the frequency and the nature of incidents that victimize students and staff associated with the five groups noted above and to identify issues and suggestions that may assist others in addressing the problem of victimization in residence halls.

Chapter III

Institutional Characteristics

INSTITUTIONAL VALUES

The means and ranges of responses to the twelve scaled items designed to assess institutional values are provided in Table 3.

TABLE 3
Institutional Values

Survey Item	Mean*	Range*
1. My institution is strongly committed to:		
Maintaining or enhancing its public image or prestige	5.9	3-7
Providing excellence in graduate/professional programs	5.5	1-7
Providing excellence in undergraduate education	5.3	2-7
Practicing affirmative action in student admissions	5.3	1-7
Providing public service	5.1	2-7
Eliminating bigotry from the campus environment	5.0	2-7
Maximizing the quality of student life outside the classroom	4.9	2-7
Practicing affirmative action in employment	4.8	1-7
Creating a multicultural campus community	4.8	2-7
Conducting research	4.8	1-7
Admitting only the highest qualified students	4.7	1-7
Meeting the needs of diverse groups of students	4.6	2-6

*Means and ranges are based on seven-point scales ranging in value from 1=Strongly Disagree to 7=Strongly Agree.

Although all means shown in Table 3 are above the midpoint on the scale provided, suggesting more agreement than disagreement overall, it is interesting to note, particularly given the problems addressed in this study, that respondents agreed most strongly with the statement involving institutional commitment to "maintaining or enhancing its public image or prestige" and expressed lowest agreement with the statement involving institutional commitment to "meeting the needs of diverse groups of students."

The greatest discrepancies in the means for public vs. private institutions showed that the public schools had greater commitment to "conducting research" (mean = 5.4 vs. 4.0) and "practicing affirmative action in employment" (mean = 5.3 vs. 4.1), and lower commitment to "admitting only the highest qualified students" (mean = 4.3 vs. 5.2).

Differences in the means according to size of the residence hall system, which is highly correlated with the size of the institution, tended to be more dramatic. For example, those in "large," "medium," and "small" categories had means of 6.1, 4.9, and 3.4, respectively, with respect to institutional commitment to "conducting research." This same pattern, showing a strong positive relationship between size and commitment (i.e., the greater the number of students, the stronger the institutional commitment), was found in reference to the following:

- providing excellence in graduate/professional programs
- maintaining or enhancing public image or prestige
- creating a multicultural campus community
- eliminating bigotry from the campus environment

STAFF TRAINING AND STUDENT PROGRAMMING REGARDING DIVERSITY ISSUES

As shown in Table 4, RAs and RDs were reported to receive similarly substantial exposure to diversity issues in their staff training programs (mean = 5.8 for both groups), but the RDs were perceived as being somewhat more sensitive to and more responsive to such issues.

It is also interesting to note that respondents were more likely to agree that programs for students are provided frequently (mean = 4.7) than they were to agree that such programs are well attended (mean = 3.6).

Respondents from large residence hall systems were substantially more likely than those from small systems to agree that staff receive a lot of information regarding diversity issues in their training programs and that diversity programs for students are presented frequently. However, perceptions of the sensitivity and responsiveness of staff and the program attendance of students are not significantly related to the size of the residence hall system.

TABLE 4
Staff Training and Student Programming

Survey Item	Mean*	Range*
2. Resident assistants (RAs) in our system are:		
Exposed to a lot of information regarding issues of diversity in their staff development/training programs	5.8	2-7
Sensitive to issues affecting minority students	5.1	2-7
Responsive to the needs and problems of diverse groups	5.2	3-7
3. Professional staff (e.g., hall directors) are:		
Exposed to a lot of information regarding issues of diversity in their staff development/training programs	5.8	2-7
Sensitive to issues affecting minority students	5.8	3-7
Responsive to the needs and problems of diverse groups	5.8	3-7
4. Residence hall programs focusing on diversity issues are:		
Provided frequently	4.7	1-7
Usually attended by many students	3.6	1-6

*Means and ranges are based on seven-point scales ranging in value from 1=Strongly Disagree to 7=Strongly Agree.

ATTITUDES AND BEHAVIORS OF STUDENTS

As noted in Table 5, agreement that many students have homophobic and sexist attitudes was stronger than agreement that they have racist and anti-Semitic attitudes. Similarly, agreement that many students engage in sexist and homophobic behaviors was stronger than agreement that they engage in racist and anti-Semitic behaviors.

Respondents were also more likely to agree that there is a lot of date rape and other violence towards women and that there is more of this violence than there was five years ago, than they were to agree that there is a lot of racial tension on campus and that there is more of this tension than there was five years ago. However, readers should note the great variability in these and other responses, which ranged from one extreme to the other on the seven-point scales provided.

TABLE 5
Student Attitudes and Behaviors

Survey Item	Mean*	Range*
5. Many of the students on this campus:		
Have homophobic (anti-gay/lesbian) attitudes	5.4	2-7
Have sexist attitudes	5.1	2-7
Have racist attitudes	4.4	2-7
Have anti-Semitic (anti-Jewish) attitudes	3.5	1-7
Engage in sexist behaviors	4.8	1-7
Engage in homophobic behaviors	4.1	1-7
Engage in racist behaviors	3.3	1-6
Engage in anti-Semitic behaviors	2.7	1-5
6. There is a lot of racial tension on our campus	3.6	1-7
There is more racial tension than there was 5 years ago	3.7	1-7
7. There is a lot of date rape and other violence toward women	4.5	1-7
There is more violence towards women than there was 5 years ago	4.0	1-7

*Means and ranges are based on seven-point scales ranging in value from 1=Strongly Disagree to 7=Strongly Agree.

INSTITUTIONAL POLICIES

Forty-eight of the 49 respondents (98%) indicated that their institutions have sexual harassment policies in effect for faculty and staff, whereas only 69% reported racial harassment policies in effect for faculty and staff. Substantially more public schools (79%) than private schools (57%) have such racial harassment policies.

Sixty percent of the respondents (including 63% of those from public schools and 57% of those from private schools) indicated that their institutions had harassment or "hate speech" policies in effect for students. Regardless of size category, private schools are slightly more likely than not to have these policies affecting students. However, 80% of the small and medium public schools, but only 42% of the large public schools have such policies.

A BRIEF SUMMARY OF ADDITIONAL FINDINGS

Most readers would logically expect to find much greater numbers of incidents of violence, vandalism, and verbal harassment in residence halls housing more than 13,000 students (i.e., at the largest school included in this study) than in residence halls housing only slightly more than 100 students (i.e., at the smallest school included in this study). The hypothesis that the number of students living in residence halls is positively correlated with the number of incidents reported in residence halls was clearly confirmed in this study.

Several statistical procedures were used to examine the relationships between the incidence of victimization in residence halls and the institutional values, staff training and student programming endeavors, student attitudes and behaviors, and institutional policies described in this chapter. However, the size of the residence hall system often served as a confounding factor, as it was significantly related to *both* the incidence of victimization and other variables of interest. Once statistical procedures "controlled for" the number of students housed in residence halls, the relationships between numbers of incidents and many other variables became non-significant.

For example, there is a significant positive correlation between perceptions of the degree of institutional commitment to "conducting research" and the number of residence hall incidents. However, it has been shown in this chapter that larger institutions are perceived to have greater commitment to research *and* that larger institutions report greater numbers of incidents. Consequently, institutions with strong commitments to research may have more incidents not because they are research-oriented, but simply because they are large.

Although further analyses may shed some light on the relationships between victimization and institutional factors, results based on preliminary analyses are inconclusive and will not be described further in this book.

Chapter IV

Incidents of Violence and Victimization In Residence Halls

INCIDENTS THAT WERE OFFICIALLY REPORTED

The *second* question in each of the 15 sets of items regarding numbers of residence hall incidents asked, "How many of these incidents were actually reported?" Table 6 shows the number of incidents reported in each of the 15 categories, along with marginal totals. The 5,526 incidents of victimization actually reported at respondent institutions included 878 incidents involving violence, 1,377 involving vandalism, and 3,271 involving verbal harassment.

TABLE 6

Numbers of Incidents Actually Reported

Student Victim Group	Violence	Vandalism	Verbal Harassment	Total
RAs	224	626	1,972	2,822
Racial/ethnic minority	141	273	259	673
Women	444	325	857	1,626
Gay/lesbian	62	131	143	336
Jewish	7	22	40	69
Totals	878	1,377	3,271	5,526

The single greatest number of total incidents (2,822) and the second greatest number of violent incidents (224) victimized RAs, even though RAs constitute only about two percent of all students reported to live in the residence halls included in this study. Indeed, when the actual number of RAs is taken into account, it becomes clear that RAs represent the group most likely to be victimized by violence in residence halls.

The second greatest number of total incidents (1,626) and the greatest number of violent incidents (444) victimized women who, as noted in Chapter II, represent approximately 51% of all residents. Racial/ethnic minority students were victimized in 673 incidents, gay/lesbian students in 336 incidents, and Jewish students in 69 incidents.

ESTIMATES OF INCIDENTS BELIEVED TO HAVE OCCURRED

The *first* question in each of the 15 sets of items asked, "In your professional judgment *(whether or not the incidents were officially reported)*, how many incidents in your residence halls during the past two years have involved [type of incident] towards [victim group]?" Not all respondents answered this question all 15 times that it was asked. Some answered in terms that were not discrete numbers. For example, the question as it pertained to violence towards women yielded responses such as, "more than you could imagine," "God only knows," "countless," and "dozens." With respect to verbal harassment of RAs, responses included "tragically, a daily occurrence in the lives of some RAs," "so many I couldn't even begin to count them all," and "literally hundreds." Because these comments and others like them could not be quantified, they could not be added to the numerical estimates provided by other respondents. Consequently, the total numbers of various types of incidents housing officers believe occurred (whether or not they were officially reported) may be considered conservative estimates.

TABLE 7

Reported Incidents as Percentages of Total Incidents Believed to Have Occurred

Student Victim Group	Violence	Vandalism	Verbal Harassment	Total
RAs	79% of 285	42% of 1,478	50% of 3,894	50% of 5,657
Racial/ethnic minority	44% of 317	34% of 805	16% of 1,579	25% of 2,701
Women	20% of 2,189	33% of 982	15% of 5,702	18% of 8,873
Gay/lesbian	23% of 265	23% of 559	16% of 906	19% of 1,730
Jewish	23% of 30	13% of 164	12% of 346	13% of 540
Totals	28% of 3,086	34% of 3,988	26% of 12,427	28% of 19,501

The figures provided in Table 7, showing the "officially reported" incidents as percentages of total incidents believed to have actually occurred, are based only on the responses of housing officers who answered both the first and second questions in the fifteen sets of items provided on the survey form.

Overall, respondents indicated that only about 28% of 19,501 total incidents believed to have occurred were ever officially reported. In the professional judgment of respondents, the reported incidents represented about 28% of 3,086 incidents of violence, 34% of 3,988 incidents of vandalism, and 26% of 12,427 incidents of verbal abuse occurring during the two-year time period in question.

Incidents victimizing RAs were perceived as being most likely to be reported. Approximately 50% of all incidents affecting RAs, but only 25% of those affecting racial/ethnic minority students, 18% of those affecting women, 19% of those affecting gay/lesbian students, and 13% of those affecting Jewish students were believed to be officially reported. Estimated reporting rates for incidents of violence were highest for RAs (79%) and lowest for women (20%), even though, as shown in Table 6, official reports of violence toward women outnumbered corresponding reports for the remaining groups.

The reporting rates for acts of vandalism were believed to be highest for incidents affecting RAs (42%) and lowest for incidents affecting Jewish students (13%). Incidents of verbal harassment perpetrated against RAs were again estimated to have the highest reporting rate (50%), while reports of verbal harassment of those in the four remaining groups were believed to represent only between 12% and 16% of such incidents.

Although the information provided in Table 7 is based on the professional judgment of housing officers, presumed to be well-informed of what actually occurs in their residence halls (whether or not information is officially reported) and in positions to offer what may be considered "educated guesses," the data in question should be clearly identified as representing *estimates only*. For that reason, *all data presented in the remainder of this chapter are based on only those incidents that were officially reported*.

IDENTIFYING OFFENDERS AND ADJUDICATING INCIDENTS

Table 8 shows that, of the 5,526 incidents that were officially reported, approximately 58% represented cases in which the offenders were identified, 50% led to disciplinary hearings, 47% led to disciplinary sanctions, and 35% led to disciplinary sanctions that respondents believed were sufficient to deter offenders from repeating similar behaviors in the future.

Offenders were identified in 81% of the violent incidents, 66% of the incidents involving verbal harassment, and only 24% of the incidents of vandalism. Perhaps because acts of vandalism (e.g., graffiti or destruction of property) are often committed when no witnesses are present, it is particularly difficult to identify the perpetrators. Table 8 suggests that, when offenders are identified and perhaps when sufficient evidence or other information is available to warrant disciplinary hearings, there is a strong probability that such hearings will yield disciplinary sanctions. However, substantial numbers of the sanctions are believed, in the professional judgment of the respondents, to be insufficient to serve as deterrents of repeated behaviors.

TABLE 8
Outcomes of Reported Incidents

Outcome	Violence	Vandalism	Verbal Harassment	Total
Note: all percentages are based on incidents actually reported (n=)	(878)	(1,377)	(3,271)	(5,526)
Offenders identified	81%	24%	66%	58%
Disciplinary hearings held	70%	22%	56%	50%
Disciplinary sanctions issued	67%	21%	53%	47%
Sanction as sufficient deterrent	48%	17%	40%	35%

For example, although approximately two-thirds (67%) of the violent incidents reported in residence halls led to the issuing of disciplinary sanctions, fewer than half (48%) of the violent incidents led to disciplinary sanctions judged by respondents to be sufficient to deter further violence.

Information provided in Table 9 (for each of the five victim groups considered separately) corresponds to that provided (for total incidents) in Table 8. Reported incidents victimizing RAs are most likely to result in disciplinary sanctions believed sufficient to deter further victimization. This is perceived to occur in reference to 45% of the reported incidents affecting RAs, 35% of the reported incidents affecting racial/ethnic minority students, 24% of the reported incidents affecting women, 23% of the reported incidents affecting Jewish students, and only 13% of the reported incidents affecting gay/lesbian students.

However, it should be noted that the percentages of reported incidents leading to disciplinary hearings, sanctions, and sanctions judged to be sufficient to serve as deterrents tend to be related to the percentages of incidents in which offenders were identified. As a result, the fact that offenders were identified in 71% of the reported incidents victimizing RAs and only 27% of the reported incidents victimizing gay and lesbian students contributes to the finding that the RA incidents were most likely and the gay/lesbian incidents were least likely to result in disciplinary sanctions judged sufficient to serve as deterrents.

TABLE 9
Outcomes of Reported Incidents (Five Victim Groups)

Outcome	Violence	Vandalism	Verbal Harassment	Total
Resident Assistants (RAs)				
Incidents reported (n=)	(224)	(626)	(1,972)	(2,822)
Offenders identified	89%	23%	84%	71%
Disciplinary hearings held	89%	20%	73%	62%
Disciplinary sanctions issued	85%	19%	68%	58%
Sanction as sufficient deterrent	69%	15%	52%	45%
Racial/Ethnic Minority Students				
Incidents reported (n=)	(141)	(273)	(259)	(673)
Offenders identified	72%	32%	48%	47%
Disciplinary hearings held	63%	31%	40%	41%
Disciplinary sanctions issued	61%	31%	39%	40%
Sanction as sufficient deterrent	51%	28%	34%	35%
Women Students				
Incidents reported (n=)	(444)	(325)	(857)	(1,626)
Offenders identified	85%	23%	37%	48%
Disciplinary hearings held	68%	23%	29%	38%
Disciplinary sanctions issued	64%	22%	28%	37%
Sanction as sufficient deterrent	40%	16%	19%	24%
Gay/Lesbian Students				
Incidents reported (n=)	(62)	(131)	(143)	(336)
Offenders identified	37%	17%	32%	27%
Disciplinary hearings held	29%	12%	24%	20%
Disciplinary sanctions issued	29%	12%	20%	18%
Sanction as sufficient deterrent	19%	8%	13%	13%
Jewish Students				
Incidents reported (n=)	(7)	(22)	(40)	(69)
Offenders identified	71%	18%	58%	46%
Disciplinary hearings held	71%	18%	48%	41%
Disciplinary sanctions issued	71%	18%	48%	41%
Sanction as sufficient deterrent	43%	9%	28%	23%

Table 9 offers a considerable amount of information that can easily be explored further by anyone with a hand calculator. For example, consider the two groups (RAs and women) affected by the greatest numbers of reported incidents of violence. In 199 (or 89%) of the 224 reported incidents of violence toward RAs, offenders were identified. Every one of these offender-identified incidents (again 89% of the total reported) led to a disciplinary hearing and 190 of them (85% of the total reported, and 95% of those in which offenders were identified and that led to hearings) yielded disciplinary sanctions. Finally, 155 incidents (69% of the total reported, 78% of those in which offenders were identified and that led to hearings, and 82% of those in which sanctions were issued) resulted in sanctions judged sufficient to serve as deterrents.

Offenders were almost as likely to be identified in reported incidents of violence against women (85%, representing 377 of the 444 reported incidents) as in reported incidents of violence against RAs (89%, as shown above). However, not all offender-identified incidents of violence against women led to disciplinary hearings. In fact, only 302 (68% of the total reported, and 80% of the incidents in which offenders were identified) did so. And although 284 of these incidents (64% of the total reported, 75% of those in which offenders were identified, and 94% of those resulting in disciplinary hearings) yielded disciplinary sanctions, only 178 of the incidents (40% of the total, 47% of those in which offenders were identified, 59% of those resulting in hearings, and 63% of those yielding sanctions) resulted in sanctions judged to be sufficient to serve as deterrents.

In summary, about 78% of violent incidents against RAs, that were reported *and* had offenders identified, led to disciplinary sanctions that respondents believed were sufficient to deter the offenders from repeating similar behaviors in the future. In contrast, only about 47% of the violent incidents against women, that were reported *and* had offenders identified, led to disciplinary outcomes judged to be sufficient to serve as deterrents.

Although campus judicial officers could undoubtedly offer many possible explanations for the above findings (e.g. lack of evidence and witnesses, "simply her word against his," etc.), such explanations were not directly explored in this study. However, the findings do seem to support commonly held assumptions regarding why women who are victims of violence do not report such violence. That is, many such women believe that, even if they do come forward to report the violence and identify the persons who perpetrated the violence against them, it is more likely than not that the offenders will be able to avoid or escape from negative consequences that might deter them from perpetrating violence against these or other women in the future. This belief undoubtedly contributes to the reluctance on the part of many women students to report acquaintance rape, courtship violence, assault, etc.

Chapter V

Descriptions of the Most Common and Most Serious Incidents

This chapter provides summaries of responses to the survey items asking housing officers to describe in one or two brief sentences "the most common type of incident" and "the most serious incident" that had victimized persons within each of the five victim groups during the past two years.

VICTIMIZATION OF RESIDENT ASSISTANTS (RAs)

Most Common Incidents

There appear to be several distinguishing features of incidents commonly victimizing RAs. First, such victimization tends to be job-related and to occur when RAs attempt to fulfill their duties associated with the enforcement of policies. Second, although some acts of vandalism are reported, the most common type of RA victimization involves verbal harassment or abuse in the form of obscene, vulgar, degrading, insulting, derogatory, belligerent, or other offensive comments. In fact, three respondents described the most common form of RA victimization simply as "verbal abuse," and three others wrote "verbal harassment." However, it appears that not all respondents considered the verbal abuse of RAs to be a form of victimization.

For example, one respondent stated, "'Victimize' is a loaded term. Probably most RAs are mouthed off at occasionally, especially if they have to take an unpopular stand. But I can only recall one instance of an RA being victimized, and that was through oral harassment because he was gay." In contrast, another respondent noted, "Verbal abuse from residents when an RA enforces policy. This does enormous damage to the RA's self confidence, especially because this comes from their peers." (Please note that the consequences of verbal harassment and other forms of victimization of RAs will be discussed further in Chapter VII.)

Third, although some written comments are noted, much of this harassment occurs orally in face-to-face situations and is directed toward individual RAs. And fourth, many incidents are related to alcohol in the sense that they occur when RAs attempt to confront violations of alcohol policies and/or when the offenders are intoxicated or otherwise under the influence of alcohol. In one case, the respondent did not specify the type of victimization, but described the most common incidents simply as "attempts to cope with intoxicated residents." Following are examples of the most common incidents:

Vandalism

- Students have put things on RAs' doors, pennied the doors, and tampered with the locks.
- Graffiti on walls, doors, signs, etc. Ripping down bulletin board info, door decorations.
- Tearing down door signs & bulletin boards, vandalism to public areas, oppressive writing on doors.
- Somebody squirts shaving cream or ketchup on their door. Students are abusive when confronted.

Verbal Harassment

- Verbal abuse from drunks!
- Alcohol related verbal harassment during a confrontation.
- Verbal harassment; general disrespect and belligerence; managing intoxicated students.
- Obscene responses to confrontation over minor behavior infractions, often caused by alcohol.
- Verbal abuse by students who feel they are being wrongly accused of violating university policy or are intoxicated.
- Verbal harassment is the most common type of incident that victimizes resident assistants. Influence of alcohol.
- Verbal harassment, most commonly of female RAs when confronting noise or underage drinking. Most often alcohol is involved. Female RAs are called "bitch" or subjected to sexually suggestive comments.
- RAs confront residents who are usually under the influence of alcohol. The residents may be uncooperative and verbally derogatory to the RA and what s/he is trying to do. On some occasions it leads into verbally abusive remarks. It almost never crosses the border to verbal threats and intimidation.
- The verbal degradation of a resident assistant by a student, either intoxicated or sober.
- Generally, staff are verbally harassed on a fairly frequent basis as a result of carrying out their responsibilities in policy enforcement. Harassment can also be found in written format; i.e., notes left on doors, in mailboxes, etc.

- Verbal harassment of an RA during and after a disciplinary incident. Most happen during an incident in the heat of the moment, with some occurring after the incident.
- Verbal harassment in response to policy enforcement, sometimes focusing on gender, race.
- Verbal harassment and prank calls.
- Most victimization occurs as verbal abuse or anonymous written messages on doors. Profanity, insults, obscenities when confronted by RAs for a rule violation.
- Calling or referring to the RA as a "bitch" or using some other vulgar word or phrase as they shut their room door.

Most Serious Incidents

The majority of respondents reported at least one act of violence toward an RA. Some RAs were physically injured (e.g., to the extent that they required stitches, reconstructive surgery, or other medical treatment) as a result of being sexually or otherwise assaulted. Although resulting injuries (if they existed) were not specified in the descriptions given by most respondents, several RAs were reported as having been hit, struck, punched, knocked to the ground, pushed or shoved up against walls, physically restrained, etc.

For many people, responding in self-defense via self-protection to an act of violence appears to be instinctive. However, one respondent described a risk staff take in such situations as follows: "A student attempted to run away from the RA, was unable to do so, and then charged (running) into the RA. The RA grabbed the student as they were colliding. The student later filed assault charges against the RA because the RA had touched the student."

Serious vandalism affecting RAs often involves their cars, one of which was actually overturned. However, it should be noted that there does not seem to be unanimous agreement regarding the extent to which damaging an RA's property and shoving an RA are to be considered "serious." For example, one respondent stated, "We've not had any truly serious incidents—some vandalizing of RA property, usually automobiles, and a couple of shoving matches."

The difference between "common verbal harassment of RAs and "serious" verbal harassment of RAs may be exemplified in the difference between "mouthing off at" or "cussing out" an RA and threatening to kill an RA, "put a bullet in [the RA's] head," or otherwise harm an RA.

As was true with the most common incidents, the most serious incidents victimizing RAs are often encountered in the line of duty, generally during disciplinary incidents or in retaliation for disciplinary actions RAs have taken. Several incidents suggest that residence hall staff may be victimized not only because they are staff, but also because they are members of the other victim groups included in this

study. For example, consider the following responses as they relate to race, gender, sexual preference, and religion:
- Penis (from a cadaver) pinned to African-American female RA's door with a note signed "KKK."
- A male student discussing rape and the "positive" aspects of rape with a female staff member when she was confronting him.
- Gay RA was orally harassed.
- A Jewish staff member's car was vandalized w/swastikas.

Other incidents described as the "most serious" ones victimizing RAs during the past two years are as follows:

Violence

- We had an RA receive stitches as a result of being punched in the face by a resident.
- RA confronting alcohol had door slammed on hand, resulting in need for reconstructive surgery.
- A resident assistant was sexually assaulted.
- RA physically shoved/hurt during an alcohol-related confrontation.
- Knocking on white female RA's door at 2 a.m. asking for help and then dragging her down hall and hitting her.
- A student doing physical harm to an RA.
- Physical assault on RAs.
- An RA was physically attacked (struck) by a resident. Resident was under the influence of alcohol and was being confronted by the RA on a policy violation.
- An RA was physically assaulted off-campus as a result of an incident of harassment which began earlier in the evening.
- An RA was hit by a friend of a current student.
- An RA (female) was knocked to the ground by some non-resident whom she had asked to leave the building.
- An RA was physically assaulted.
- While attempting to monitor a social event, being physically accosted by non-students who were "crashing the party."
- An RA was pushed up against a wall by an angry student.
- An RA (female) was pushed against a wall by an intoxicated man while other male students gathered and supported the man's actions.
- A student pushing an RA against a wall. The RA was not physically injured.
- RA who was shoved several times while dealing with an intoxicated student.

- A push or shove upon confronting a situation—no overt physical contact however.
- An RA was physically held by the student during a confrontation.

Vandalism
- Windows were broken in his suite.
- Vandalism to car.
- Most serious property damage was overturning an RA's car.

Verbal Harassment
- A student threatened to "put a bullet in your head." Same student later went on to explain that he was in a fascist organization and would get the RA.
- A resident told an RA he wouldn't live to regret anything the RA did to the resident.
- The life of an RA was threatened.
- Threat of personal violence by a resident to a staff member.
- Threat of physical violence.
- A group of intoxicated residents and non-residents were in a floor lounge after midnight. When the RA tried to disperse the group they refused to disperse and verbally abused the RA and verbally threatened to do physical harm to him.
- Threat by drunken guests of student . . . to physically abuse the RA. No actual physical violence has occurred in the past two years.
- A staff member had something obscene written on her message board.
- Most serious "mental damage" was putting up derogatory signs all over the building about an RA.
- Verbal abuse from other RAs in front of students.

Combined, Non-Specific, and Other Incidents
- RAs being assaulted by non-students. Verbal abuse during a confrontation situation; RA may have been shoved or hit. Students taking out frustration on RA as a title, not a person.
- Constant harassment by group of women, but not enough to charge judicially.
- Concerted effort by several students on one floor to "oust" the RA because he was not turning his back on their continuing rules violations.

VICTIMIZATION OF WOMEN
Most Common Incidents

Incidents described as the "most common" ones victimizing women differ from those affecting all other victim groups in the sense that a disproportionate number of them involve acts of violence (e.g., rape, battering, and courtship violence). In contrast to the verbal harassment of RAs, most often directed toward specific RAs orally in face-to-face situations, the verbal harassment of women is often covert (e.g., anonymous written messages, obscene phone calls, graffiti, and posting of pornographic photos or offensive cartoons), sexually explicit or sexually suggestive, and directed toward women in general (or toward specific women purely because of their membership in this group). Following are examples of "the most common type of incident" victimizing women.

Violence
- Rape.
- Acquaintance rape. (2 responses)
- Date rape.
- Date rape plus influence of alcohol in some cases.
- Relationship violence.
- Physical abuse by a male "friend." Battering.
- Courtship violence.
- Male students hitting female dating partners.

Vandalism
- Graffiti about women, body parts, etc.
- Writings/depictions on their room doors.

Verbal Harassment
- Mostly covert type incidents. Posting of pornographic photos, etc. not directed at an individual woman, but women in general.
- Pictures, cartoons, words on male students' doors.
- "Hate" messages.
- Written & verbal harassment by male students, verbal assault.
- Yelling obscenities out of windows towards women.
- Man yelling obscenities at his girlfriend when aggravated. Loud enough disturbance to motivate RA to go to room and intervene.
- Male guest verbally harassing roommates or floormates of students they are visiting.
- Verbal harassment—catcalls, whistles, comments, etc.
- Women who are called names such as "bitch" or the target of suggestive sexual remarks.
- Obscene comments being directed at women.
- Oral harassment, name-calling (e.g., "bitch," "cunt").
- Phone calls and verbal harassment from ex-boyfriends.
- Verbal harassment, especially obscene phone calls.

- The most prevalent form of victimization of women students seems to be telephone harassment. The number of cases is dramatically increasing.
- Obscene, unidentified, repeat phone calls.
- Harassing phone calls.
- Telephone harassment.
- Derogatory "jokes."

Combined, Non-Specific, and Other Incidents
- Date rape/sexual harassment.
- Women who attend unsanctioned gatherings that involve alcohol and are sexually harassed verbally and physically.
- Usually a verbal abuse situation; occasionally physical contact of a limited sort.
- Arguments between couples.
- Domestic situations between dating couples.
- Drunken men who want sex with them.
- The most common type of incident that victimizes women students in our residence hall system is that a woman will go to a party, most likely off-campus, and either receive peer pressure to drink alcohol or be given punch-type drinks loaded with hard alcohol. The intoxicated woman will then return to the halls and may find herself in compromising sexual situations, the nature of the behavior contrary to the usual behavior of that woman.
- The attitude of total disregard for the rights of women—viewing them as "less than" men in every respect.

Most Serious Incidents

Almost all respondents indicated that the "most serious" incidents victimizing women involved some form of violence. More than half of all incidents reported involved rape (sexual assault). Many other incidents of violence involved physical assault or battery. The frequent use of terms such as "acquaintance rape," "date rape," "relationship violence," or "courtship violence" suggest that most women were victimized by violence perpetrated by men they knew. Some were victimized by more than one crime (e.g., being kidnapped and raped or being beaten and raped). A sampling of the most serious incidents victimizing women follows:

Violence
- Date rape. (4 responses)
- Acquaintance rape. (2 responses)
- Date/acquaintance rape.
- Rape, date rape.

- Rape.
- Sexual assault. Date rape.
- Sexual assault/rape.
- Rape by an unknown assailant.
- A woman was kidnapped and brutally raped.
- A woman was raped in a man's residence hall room. They had a "passing" acquaintance. The man is serving a 10-year sentence in prison, after plea-bargaining to a lesser charge.
- The reported acquaintance rapes—especially one involving a senior who raped a woman in her first week at school.
- Date rape situation which involved sexual assaults from various members of a fraternity.
- Date rape plus influence of alcohol in most cases.
- Date rape in which male student took advantage of female's being intoxicated.
- Sexual assault.
- A number of women have been sexually assaulted while in the residence halls.
- Woman beaten and sexually assaulted by a man she was dating.
- Physical abuse and date rape.
- The two most serious incidents involving the victimization of women students are: (1) an acquaintance rape in the hall where the woman was a friend of the attacker, and (2) a woman was physically abused by her boyfriend in the hall.
- Woman assaulted in bathroom on her own female floor, by males.
- Several different instances of physical assault.
- Woman assaulted by boyfriend; refused to pursue any charges.
- A female student assaulted by her boyfriend off-campus. We don't have much happen in the halls themselves, but deal with the aftermath.
- A man choking and threatening a woman and then losing control with residence staff and public safety officers.
- Throwing a woman down a flight of concrete steps—both parties were on drugs during the confrontation.
- A male student hit his pregnant girlfriend repeatedly in the abdomen.
- A male non-student physically assaulted his girlfriend to the point where she was taken to the hospital.
- Male angry at female strikes female causing physical injury.
- Women in violence situations.

Verbal Harassment
- Anonymous threats of physical assault.
- 2 month "fascination" & phone nuisance of 1st year nursing student.
- Pornographic photo with the face of a woman student pasted over photo with her phone number printed below, which was then posted at various places around campus.

Combined, Non-Specific, and Other Incidents
- Relationship violence issues with harassment, damage to property, intimidating environment for the female with her feeling as though she has no control. The university is often able to do very little due to lack of evidence and "loopholes" in the law.
- We had an instance of alleged date rape last year between residents. In [this state] the law dictates there must be penetration by some object for rape to have occurred. That didn't happen in this case but the woman continues to "feel" she was raped to this day.
- Consistent harassment behavior from identified individuals involved in slow-moving discipline process.

VICTIMIZATION OF RACIAL / ETHNIC MINORITY STUDENTS

Most Common Incidents

Incidents most commonly victimizing racial/ethnic minority students fall into the category of verbal harassment and often take the form of racial slurs or epithets. Just as the verbal harassment of women focused on their gender, the verbal harassment of minority students focuses on their race or ethnicity. In comparison to incidents of verbal harassment of RAs, there are fewer cases of face-to-face verbal exchanges based on specific actions that may have made the offenders angry, and more subversive and anonymous incidents (e.g., graffiti, written messages, or defacement of materials on bulletin boards) directed toward individuals or groups purely on the basis of their racial/ethnic identity.

Only two respondents described acts of violence as the "most common" incidents. One described "fights among black and non-black students," and the other described "verbal abuse and some fights between racial groups which always involve drunks." Several respondents described subtle forms of victimization associated with prejudice and discrimination (e.g., "cold shoulders" or avoidance of, insensitivity to, lack of inclusion of, and differential treatment of racial/ethnic minorities). These examples are listed within the "combined, non-specific, and other" category following a sampling of incidents of vandalism and verbal harassment.

Vandalism
- Vandalism to cars.
- Graffiti.
- Vandalism, racial slurs on bulletin board or student doors or in hallway.
- Vandalism to bulletin boards pertaining to racial/ethnic topics.
- Racial slurs written/painted on walls, doors or bulletin boards.
- Defacing doors/bulletin boards with racial comments.

Verbal Harassment
- Name calling.
- Verbal assault.
- Usually verbal epithets.
- Racial/ethnic slurs.
- Racial slurs whispered as a student goes by.
- Comments made as a student walks by or comments made in a room intended to be heard by someone outside the room.
- Verbal degradation of a student who is a racial/ethnic minority.
- Racial slurs ... usually stated in situations involving anger.
- Harassment and use of name calling in the heat of anger.
- Usually a slur about a practice, song, class, etc.
- We have only one case of verbal harassment thus far. There seems to be a reluctance or unwillingness to report incidents of this nature. Written/verbal slurs.
- Students make unwitting or casual comments based on lack of experience in dealing with students of color that would be interpreted as being racist, or at least insensitive.
- Ethnic intimidation through inappropriate posters, flyers degrading a specific ethnic group.
- Racist messages on doors, bulletin boards, or computer network.
- Hate messages on doors.
- Anonymous harassing phone calls.

Combined, Non-Specific, and Other Incidents
- Verbal harassment/roommate difficulties. Verbal and written slurs. Ethnic comments, stereotypical derogatory statements.
- Writing in the restrooms and some roommate conflicts.
- The most common incident would be roommate complaints at the beginning of the year, based on the race of the roommate.
- Anonymous verbal harassment; also, "cold shoulders" from the surrounding community (small town, rural, white, ...).

- Societal outcasts—treated differently due to small numbers.
- Insensitivity to different needs, customs, ... lifestyles.
- Most incidents are subtle forms of "discriminatory" treatment such as inclusion (or lack of) in floor or hall activities.
- Just plain being ignored or not included.
- Hard looks, silences, moving away.
- There simply haven't been any violent acts directed toward minorities. However, I believe some of their theft problems are racially motivated.

Most Serious Incidents

Many incidents of violence reported in this category are described as "fights" or other types of physical confrontations. Although respondents indicated that several of these incidents were preceded by racial slurs, threats, or other verbal exchanges, they are included within the "violence" category below. It should perhaps be noted that the majority of the "most serious" incidents victimizing racial/ethnic minority students involved verbal harassment or vandalism that did *not* lead to violence. Following are some examples:

Violence

- White attacked an Alaskan native for no apparent reason. However, both individuals were drunk.
- A group of white students harassing a group of African-Americans through vandalism led to a physical altercation with one student brandishing a hammer.
- Slurs that developed into fist fights.
- Racial comments were yelled at black student, which resulted in a near riot.
- Fighting.
- An assistant hall director and student security worker were called racial names to their faces, which led to a physically violent situation.
- African-American woman being verbally harassed and physically pushed around by 5 white males.
- A Caucasian student called an African-American male student "boy." A black female RA became enraged. Racial slurs were exchanged. The female acted out violently by throwing an item at the Caucasian student. No one was physically injured.
- An ethnic minority student was called out of the building to participate in a physical altercation.
- Physical assault.
- Verbal and physical harassment of minority student.

- One [student] was hit, but I do not believe it was race related.
- A fight involving four white students and two black students. It wasn't clearly racially motivated, but I believe that and alcohol were big factors.
- Fight between black and white intramural basketball teams.

Vandalism
- Vandalism to a flyer on Afro-American students' door telling them to "go back to Africa."
- Vandalism to car.
- A minority RA was harassed through abuse of property and in writing by a fellow resident who was white.
- Ongoing harassment (written notes) and eggs on door.

Verbal Harassment
- Student approached by gang of white males and threatened with violence (was not beaten—public safety arrived to intervene).
- "Most severe" are mostly verbal, confrontive situations with no violence. Our staff usually intervene before it gets physical.
- Students were called *niggers* and then threatened with bodily harm.
- Threatening speech / intimidating body stance.
- Racial comments which were demeaning to the individual.
- A student was subjected to racial slurs by her roommate in the heat of an argument about differences in living together.
- A note was left for a black female student referring to her in a derogatory manner and asking her to leave.
- Oppressive language used. Example: "I hate niggers."
- Racial slurs: written and verbal.
- Various symbols that offend.

Combined, Non-Specific, and Other Incidents
- Two black students approached by "skin heads."
- Harassment for dating a person from a different culture.
- A dead animal was thrown into a room.
- Ongoing harassment that drives students of color to withdraw from our universities.
- This incident involves a form of victimization of a group of students. Student employees of a hall reception desk met on their own to discuss ways to "control" black students who congregate in lobby to talk, listen to music, socialize. Student employees were asked, after we learned of their meeting, to meet again to discuss issue. Inservice was planned to sensitize group.

VICTIMIZATION OF GAY/LESBIAN STUDENTS

Most Common Incidents

Gay/lesbian students appear to be most commonly victimized by written comments, particularly in the form of graffiti. Oral comments take the form of jokes and homophobic terminology (derogatory words used in reference to homosexuals) and are often made when gay/lesbian students are not present (or not known to be present).

It is interesting to note that several respondents indicated that incidents victimizing gay and lesbian students do not occur or are not known to occur in their residence halls. For example, responses included: "Since this is a Catholic university, this issue is underground"; "Our campus is not very open to gay/lesbian students, ... [so they] are not very visible"; "The problem is underground, very few problems because few residence hall students are out"; and "Very closed situation, no incidents reported." Examples of the most common types of victimization that were described by other respondents are as follows:

Vandalism
- Anti-gay graffiti.
- Name calling / graffiti.
- "Kill Fags" is often the graffiti of choice.
- Anti-gay/lesbian graffiti.
- Graffiti on a resident's door.
- Harassment by students on the floor by doing things to the gay student's door.
- Defacing/ripping down publicity put up by our gay/lesbian student organization.
- Tearing down or defacing flyers announcing G/L student meetings.
- When putting on programs related to this topic, students write derogatory comments on posters.

Verbal Harassment
- Verbal abuse.
- Verbal epithets.
- Degrading remarks.
- Homophobic statements and slurs.
- Vile messages on the computer system.
- Anonymously hung signs identifying certain students as being affiliated with ... (our bi-sexual-gay-lesbian student organization). Also, notes sent thru campus mail.
- Anti-gay comment among groups who are unaware that these groups contain gay students.

- Comments in hall about students' alleged sexual preferences.
- General derogatory remarks based on perceived sexual orientation.
- Jokes.
- Jokes, use of defamatory language even in casual conversation ("faggot," "dyke").

Combined, Non-Specific, and Other Incidents

- Gay/lesbian/bisexual students are most often victimized by devaluing/oppressive/homophobic notes on their room doors, graffiti on their floors, etc. Students experience harassing phone calls and have other students refer to them as "fags, dykes, and queers."
- Combination of "petty" vandalism and continual verbal harassment.
- Name calling and writing on doors.
- The most common type of incident that victimizes gay or lesbian students in our residence hall system is when a known homosexual couple is marginalized and discussed among the other members of the floor. What usually happens is that derogatory remarks are made within earshot of the couple. Almost universally, this couple is not included in the mainstream functioning of the floor or hall.
- Not so much an incident, but rather the general environment which includes jokes, name calling or derogatory names for gays, lesbians and bisexuals used in general conversation.
- Lack of understanding.
- Roommate situations where the heterosexual wants to move.

Most Serious Incidents

Only a few of the "most serious" incidents victimizing gay/lesbian students involved acts of physical violence. Rather, these incidents tend to be associated with "taunting" or "tormenting" gay/lesbian students via ongoing verbal harassment and vandalism. Respondents indicated that several students had moved out of the residence hall or withdrawn from school as a result of this harassment.

Because so much of the harassment included both vandalism and verbal harassment, occasionally combined with other crimes such as theft and extortion, many incidents are listed within the "combined, non-specific, and other" category. In addition, it should be noted that some respondents again emphasized, for example, that "homophobia is prevalent; hence, no gay/lesbian students speak out." Consequently, even serious incidents may seldom be reported. Examples of incidents that did come to the attention of respondents include the following:

Violence
- Assault.
- Student attacked in the shower.

- A male student assaulted by another male student because the victim was gay—no prior interaction had occurred between the two.
- Violent outburst by roommate when he discovered his roommate was gay.
- Fist fight w/name calling.

Vandalism
- Graffiti.
- Chalk anti-gay writing on sidewalks and buildings.
- Obscene graffiti written on room door.
- Harassment by students on the floor by doing things to the gay student's door.
- Someone urinated under the door to his room.

Verbal Harassment
- Threatening bodily harm to a student.
- Anonymous threats.
- Two students had to move across campus because they were being verbally harassed continually in their hall. It was "suspected" that they were gay.
- One male student faced ongoing harassment including non-stop harassing telephone calls, vandalism, signs about the student were posted everywhere. Offender was not identified and student withdrew from school.
- Student who "came out" was harassed by phone calls.
- Phone harassment, signs on doors, etc.
- The most serious incident involving a homosexual occurred when a young male, comfortable with his homosexuality, was very open about this on the residence hall floor. A group of about three or four male residents made life difficult for this person through tormenting activity that included: derogatory remarks to his face, similar notes appearing on his door, pictures of naked women appearing on his door, and derogatory phone calls made to his room.
- [Signs] were hung on every student door on a floor in an all-women's residence. A note was left in the bathroom, listing each student's name and an indication of whether the student was "straight" or a lesbian. Perpetrators had anonymously phoned dean of students 2 weeks earlier to complain of a lesbian resident.

Combined, Non-Specific, and Other Incidents
- Students chased and threatened by other residents.
- Verbal threats and vandalism to a student's door.
- A lesbian experienced harassing notes on her door. She was ignored and avoided by other students. In one incident her clothing was shred-

ded. She was addressed with hateful comments. A group of students banded together and demanded that the RHD kick the lesbian out of the hall.
- Extortion based on perceived sexual orientation/cross dressing. Constant verbal, written harassment of two students until they moved out.
- Roommate intimidating, threatening, stealing from gay male.
- A resident showing a confided statement of his roommate's being gay to the entire house. The house then "driving" the student to transfer to another building.
- Taunting.
- One resident was harassed and had to move out (anonymous perpetrator).
- A gay male was excluded from floor community activities.
- Labeling a student as gay.

VICTIMIZATION OF JEWISH STUDENTS

Most Common Incidents

As was true in reference to gay/lesbian students, several respondents indicated that there have been no incidents in their residence halls that have victimized Jewish students. Some indicated that this was because no Jewish students or very few Jewish students are enrolled at their institutions, particularly those affiliated with Catholic or other Christian denominations. Others suggested that there were significant numbers of Jewish students (and staff) on their campuses and that, as a result, considerable positive attention was given to their religious orientation. For example, one respondent stated, "We get Jewish holidays off here. There is understanding and acceptance of this population."

Oral comments (whether or not directed at or stated in the presence of someone known to be Jewish) appear to reflect ignorance and insensitivity, as opposed to anger or hatred. Anti-Semitism is perhaps most often expressed in the form of graffiti. In such cases, a symbol (as opposed to words) is generally used. And that symbol is a swastika. Sample responses are as follows:

Vandalism
- Graffiti, swastika.
- Swastikas.
- Verbal harassment—written on students' doors.

Verbal Harassment
- Verbal slurs.
- Verbal harassment.
- Verbal epithets

- Verbal assault.
- Anti-Semitic comments in context of other discussion.
- Verbal slurs—going to "Jewtown."
- Some occasional written material—context is general and not directed at any individual.
- Flippant comments; inappropriate references.
- Uneducated statements about Jewish people. Stereotypic jokes occur about Jewish people.
- A statement being made to a Jewish student that they have "all the money" and do not need financial aid.
- Jokes told about Jewish people.
- To no Jewish person in particular, the most common type of incident that victimizes Jewish students is when a casual, unwitting joke is told by a resident to a group of residents.

Combined, Non-Specific, and Other Incidents
- Graffiti or slurs (directed at Jews in general rather than a specific person).
- Common use of "JAP." Swastikas visible.
- Lack of attention to holidays and religious rituals.
- Presumption of Christianity, especially at holiday times.
- Insensitive ignorance.

Most Serious Incidents

Many respondents indicated that there had been no serious incidents victimizing Jewish students in their residence halls during the past two years. Two incidents would be categorized as "violent." Most of the remaining responses described verbal harassment or vandalism, particularly graffiti showing swastikas.

Violence
- A mid-eastern student (male) held down a Jewish student (male) and drew on his body with a magic marker. Among the things he drew on his body was a swastika.
- Students physically and verbally assaulted.

Vandalism
- A swastika was painted on a basement wall.
- Jewish students who had swastikas drawn on their door.
- Anti-Semitic remarks and graffiti on bulletin boards.
- A swastika being placed on a Jewish student's door.
- Swastika and derogatory statements on door.
- Verbal harassment—written on students' doors.

Verbal Harassment
- Anonymous threats.
- Anti-Semitic, pro-Nazi remarks aimed at Jewish students.
- Written comments in a "hate letter" from group of students.
- Written derogatory remarks.
- Name calling—jokes.
- Jokes.

Combined, Non-Specific, and Other Incidents
- A roommate situation ... Their differences were personal, not religious, but the floor interpreted the differences as religious and the roommate did not discourage it.
- T-shirts for sale: "Slap a JAP."

SUMMARY

The victimization of RAs is clearly job-related, generally occurs during or following a disciplinary incident, and often involves the use or abuse of alcohol. The most common incidents victimizing RAs tend to take the form of face-to-face verbal abuse, while the most serious incidents involve acts of violence ranging from physically restraining or pushing and shoving an RA to attacking, hitting, or otherwise assaulting an RA to the extent that medical attention is needed.

Violence, particularly in the forms of date/acquaintance rape and courtship/relationship violence, was involved in almost all of the "most serious" incidents victimizing women, as well as in a substantial number of the "most common" incidents victimizing women in residence halls. In addition, many of the incidents of vandalism and verbal harassment perpetrated against women (e.g., obscene phone calls, pornographic postings, and offensive comments yelled from windows) were specifically related to their sexuality.

The group appearing to be most willing to respond to "hate speech," threats, and violence by "fighting back" are racial/ethnic minority students. However, it should be clearly stated that, although many of the incidents resulting in racial violence began at the verbal level, most of the verbal abuse and vandalism perpetrated against minority students did *not* result in violence. Rather, minority students, along with gay/lesbian students and Jewish students, bear the burden of being continuously victimized by offensive, taunting, tormenting behaviors on the part of other students. Although some may be tempted to define incidents of vandalism and verbal harassment as "minor," it is emphasized that words like "nigger," and symbols like swastikas cause pain and suffering to many students who perceive their residence hall and campus environments not only as cold, unwelcoming, and insensitive, but as downright hostile and intimidating. Such environments are clearly far from the ideal ones that would be conducive to the learning, growth, and development of our students.

So, *what can we do* to prevent the occurrence of the types of incidents described in this chapter and most effectively address such incidents of victimization in the event that they do occur on our campuses and in our residence halls? This question and some of the many possible answers to it will be explored in the next two chapters.

Chapter VI

Suggestions and Issues Identified by Housing Officers

The last two free-response items pertaining to each of the five victim groups asked respondents to describe (1) suggestions they would offer to other housing officers and (2) issues that should be explored further within the housing profession in relation to preventing or addressing issues of victimization. Respondents were also encouraged to attach additional comments if they wished to do so.

Many respondents took advantage of this opportunity and submitted between one handwritten page and ten typewritten, single-spaced pages of comments. The sheer volume of commentary concerning victimization in residence halls and the lack of signed consent to quote some of the more institution-specific comments clearly prohibit full disclosure of all responses via word-for-word quotations in this report. Consequently, these responses will be summarized.

Several common themes permeate the issues, suggestions, and other comments offered with respect to victimization of *all five groups* identified in this study. These themes focus on the following areas:

INSTITUTIONAL AND PERSONAL VALUES

Respondents emphasized affirmation of the human value, human dignity, and human rights of all individuals and all sub-groups of students and staff on our campuses. It was recommended that such affirmation be clearly articulated in public statements issued by institutional leaders and in student handbooks or other institutional publications. Further, respondents indicated that such affirmation should be clearly reflected in institutional policies, admissions and hiring practices, staff training programs, student programs, and counseling and disciplinary procedures.

"The *values* of the institution that include respect for all persons are critical." Several respondents suggested that values inherent in academic communities should call into question some values perceived to be commonly accepted in our larger society and provide examples of communities where "tolerance and respect for others is emphasized." For example, it was noted that: "*society* is a problem here"; that "racism is everywhere"; that "sexism is widely accepted as a normal part of our culture"; that we are exposed to numerous public examples of women who are presented as "LESS THAN"; that "homophobia is rampant"; and that we should "not be fooled by the relative tolerance [for Jewish people] in contemporary U. S. society."

Some suggestions that housing officers participating in this study indicated they would make to their professional colleagues are that: they and their "senior administrators" make an effort to "look inward"; "reflect on their own values regarding diversity"; "evaluate their own attitudes and conduct"; "examine their own behavior and attitudes"; "educate themselves on gay/lesbian/bisexual issues"; "learn more about the long history and cycle of oppression of Jews"; become "sensitized to heterosexist language"; and "examine their own attitudes and language (especially off the job)."

Respondents suggested that the values of institutional leaders, often interpreted as the values of the institution itself, are projected in public statements, demonstrated commitment to affirmative action, willingness to financially support (and attend) staff/faculty workshops concerning diverse populations, providing a forum for discussion of relevant issues, "mentoring" or being an "ally" of or "advocate" for minority group members, and "taking victimization seriously."

One respondent indicated that we should "re-examine our approach to [diversity] issues," and noted that "our biggest problem is that no one (outside the members of these groups) sees these issues as important until after something happens." Respondents suggested that housing officers and other administrators: "take 'minor' racial incidents seriously before you end up with 'major' racial incidents on your hands"; "take homophobia seriously"; "take the victimization of women seriously; lose the 'boys will be boys' philosophy," and "stop accepting alcohol as an excuse for what is clearly unacceptable behavior."

It was recommended that administrators who have high visibility and strong influence on the campus: "actively role-model" positive behaviors; "take public stands"; make it clear that "*isms* have no place in higher education"; emphasize that "acts of bigotry will not be tolerated"; and "use moral persuasion" to create campus communities in which understanding, acceptance, and respect predominate.

POLICIES

Policy issues identified most often by respondents are those associated with harassment policies, staff policies, alcohol policies, and weapons policies. The primary suggestions are that policy statements be very clear; that they outline not only the policy, but also procedures for enforcing the policy, procedures for confronting and adjudicating incidents in which the policy is violated, and the disciplinary sanctions or other possible consequences associated with policy violations; and that they be well-communicated to all students, staff, and faculty throughout the institution.

Harassment Policies

Some respondents support the development of "a written policy against *any* type of harassment," or an "all-inclusive" harassment policy that focuses on the various forms of harassment itself, as opposed to the people who are most likely to be harassed. For example, "be very, very upfront regarding consequences for this behavior, regardless of *who* is victimized. Don't single out RA staff."

In contrast, several other respondents recommended: that "high risk" victim groups be clearly identified (e.g., in a "strong sexual harassment policy"; "a section of the code that deals specifically with sexual assault"; "a specific racial harassment policy in the student conduct code"; harassment policies that include "sexual orientation" and "religious preferences"; and "explicit policies about the treatment of all employees, including RAs").

One respondent said that "we shouldn't have to tell" students that it is against the rules to verbally or physically assault a university employee, but although such a rule may seem intuitively reasonable to housing or other administrators, several respondents seemed to endorse the statement made by one: "make sure your conduct code offers protection for staff members against harassment or abuse."

Many respondents emphasized that policy statements should include the descriptions of consequences that will result if policies are violated. One person indicated that consequences for certain violations should be "automatic," while others seemed to believe that specific circumstances surrounding incidents warrant case-by-case consideration. One recommended that sanctions stated in the policy itself be described as ranging "up to and including dismissal from the university." One believed institutions should make it clear (in writing) that it is their policy, "whenever appropriate or necessary, to make referrals for civil action and/or criminal prosecution." (Please note that sanctions will be discussed further in *Adjudicating Incidents* section.)

It was noted that written policies are generally ineffective unless or until they are regularly communicated and consistently enforced. It was recommended that diversity statements or harassment policies be clearly articulated in writing and be published not only in a student handbook, but in residence hall materials. Further, it was suggested that such policies be summarized in public (oral or written) statements made by institutional or housing leaders, in faculty/staff orientation sessions, in materials appropriate for posting on residence hall bulletin boards, at floor or hall meetings, and in discussions with student government or other student groups.

One respondent suggested an outline of procedures to follow ("so the left hand will know what the right hand will do") in the event that victimization occurs. One recommended "a program or policy that will send staff through a step-by-step process when harassment of any sort is reported." It was suggested that "intervention plans" include not only disciplinary actions involving the offenders, but "victim support," and "counseling services, medical treatment, or whatever else is necessary" to assist victims. Finally, it was recommended that both policies and their corresponding sets of procedures be "firmly in place before they have to be implemented." "Plan ahead. Try to prevent these things from happening, but be prepared to deal with them if they do happen."

Several issues were noted in reference to harassment policies. There appears to be some concern that one's "hands are tied" in developing and implementing policies regarding harassment at the verbal level, and requests were made for: conference presentations or publications dealing with first amendment issues as they relate to "hate speech policies"; a sharing of written harassment policies among institutions, "a monograph on how schools handle cases of harassment or violence"; a summary of "what other schools are doing about telephone harassment"; and "discussions regarding sexual harassment and sexual assault policies on various campuses—review them and discuss implementing, publicizing and adjudicating them."

Another issue involves the jurisdiction of housing policies outside of the residence halls and institutional policies in the off-campus environment. Although the following quotation involves RAs specifically, the issue itself extends to other victims.

- An issue that has arisen is the RA's jurisdiction and parameters regarding a resident's intimidation. What often may happen is that an RA, days, weeks, or even months following an incident may be confronted and intimidated by the resident. Very likely in this scenario, this intimidation may occur outside the boundaries of the university at a party, bar, shopping mall, etc.

It was suggested that housing officers and other institutional officials discuss what they wish the jurisdiction of their policies to be and what such jurisdiction can or must be, in light of federal legislation and state and local laws. In addition, a need was expressed for further discussions of the Campus Security Act and the Drug-Free Schools and Communities Act as they affect housing staff, residence hall policies, etc.

Staff Policies

Most of the policies specifically related to staff emphasized affirmative action in recruiting and hiring practices and responsibilities or liabilities of institutions as employers with respect to the victimization of their employees.

Although recommendations that housing officers "begin with recruitment of a diverse and/or racially sensitive staff"; "strongly advocate affirmative action policies" and "demonstrate support of affirmative action in hiring policies at all staff levels" were also made in reference to racial/ethnic, gender, and religious groups, the comments chosen to serve as examples in this section pertain to sexual orientation:

- Gay/lesbian/bisexual students deserve role models. University environments must communicate the value of their many gay/lesbian/bisexual faculty and staff members. These individuals need to be empowered to be positive role models for our students.
- Recruiting more "out" gays and lesbians to positions of power, prestige, leadership.
- Try to have gay/lesbian/bisexual staff to provide people that gay/lesbian/bisexual students can talk with. Also, encourage staff to be "out" as allies.
- First step: environment should be supportive of gay/lesbian staff.
- It's been helpful to have openly gay, lesbian & bisexual RAs and professional staff.

Professional activities related to gay/lesbian staff issues include "research on the victimization of this group and including this group when discussing diversity or multicultural issues"; information regarding "coming out in the professional world"; and "extending the discussion of professional live-in staff who have a partner who would also like to live in." Difficulty in demonstrating support for gay/lesbian staff and students within states having legislation that is non-supportive of gay rights was also noted.

One respondent said that the professional association for housing officers "must role-model commitment to this lifestyle." One respondent asked, "Is the organization open to gay and lesbian professionals?" Others appeared to believe that was the case (e.g., "I think ACUHO-I is doing well through conference programs; a gay, lesbian, bisexual committee; the annual reception; etc.").

Another issue concerns sensitivity to the needs of diverse staff once they are hired. For example, title VII of the Civil Rights Act (42 U.S.C. 2000[d] with regulations at 34 C.F.R. 100) requires employers to make reasonable accommodations with respect to religious practices. One respondent noted the dilemma faced by "Orthodox Jewish staff required to work on the highest holy days"; one suggested that on-duty assignments be adjusted whenever possible to accommodate religious practices; and one recommended that housing officers "pay attention to Jewish holidays when scheduling events" such as RA training.

One issue discussed by several respondents involves "employee rights and expectations in cases of victimization." For example, should institutions "make reparations for damages done to staff belongings (i.e., cars and other personal property)?" To what extent do institutional insurance policies and "workers' compensation parameters" apply to RAs or other staff who are injured "in the line of duty?" What is the institution's "legal liability" or "moral responsibility" with respect to such injury?

What is the employer's "legal responsibility to an RA who was involved in a situation where he/she failed to follow appropriate procedures (e.g., struck a student in retaliation)?" And should an institution's legal counsel defend staff members accused of inappropriate behaviors (versus acts of self-defense) when "who pushed whom first" is not clear?

It was recommended that staff (as well as students) be informed of their rights and be encouraged to report incidents in which their rights or the rights of others have been violated. For example, several respondents noted that some RAs accept verbal harassment "as part of daily life" and do not report it unless it reaches intolerable levels or "until it truly gets out of hand." Similarly, some RAs seem accepting of minor acts of vandalism "until it affects their cars" or otherwise becomes expensive. A few even "brush off" incidents of violence "as long as it stays at the pushing and shoving level." One respondent emphasized that, "we need to inform the RA of his/her legal rights as a person."

Several emphasized the importance of developing, communicating, and enforcing policies protecting staff and suggested that we can best assure RAs of our support and encourage RAs to report incidents of victimization by addressing incidents that are reported in an effective manner:

- Make it clear that harassment or any interference of staff will not be tolerated. This is done by presenting a clear message proactively, but also by dealing with violations in a firm, consistent and expeditious manner.

- The university must be aggressive about such instances in order to maintain morale by protecting the staff. Our students know that they are jeopardizing their future if they physically touch any of our staff or harass them in other ways. We respond strongly to verbal situations as well, although the staff tend to be more forgiving of verbal harassment or threats that occur during an incident.

- Developing a continuing support system for RAs. Providing strong support from the "top" of the system. RAs need to report it. It needs to be taken seriously by all college officials—as a disruption of their ability to do their jobs.

- The matter should be handled at the highest level of the discipline process to underscore its seriousness. The process should be followed to the letter, with the student seeing in the formality the seriousness of the institution. If guilt is established, serious sanctions ought to be imposed.
- Keep asking what you would do if it was a non-RA who was victimized. Remember, the other RAs will be watching how you handle the situation. It could help their sense of backing/support if dealt with properly—cannot afford to impact staff morale negatively.

Alcohol and Weapons Policies

The two types of additional policies mentioned most often are those involving alcohol and weapons. One respondent recommended that housing officers "re-establish and enforce strict behavior standards and get rid of alcohol." Several noted the common relationship between incidents of victimization and the use or abuse of alcohol and suggested that "we must come to grips with the alcohol problem if we want to solve other problems that are directly or indirectly caused by alcohol."

Two respondents expressed concern for increased numbers of incidents involving weapons, particularly handguns. In neither case was a shooting reported, but the possession of guns in residence halls and threats to use such guns "if necessary" were suggested as "serious discussion topics for our entire profession nowadays."

STAFF TRAINING

Suggestions for staff training were numerous, in part because staff must understand and communicate institutional and residence hall policies, confront and report violations of such policies, be sensitive to the needs and issues affecting diverse student populations, identify the potential for the victimization of others and address such victimization if it occurs, and be prepared to deal with the fact that they, too, (staff) can be and often are victimized.

Although most suggestions pertain to RAs and other live-in staff, many respondents acknowledged that they, too, have educational needs pertaining to the topics addressed in this study. For example, they expressed interest in professional activities concerning "how to establish yourself as a minority advocate"; "the social identity development of gay/lesbian students"; "Jewish oppression throughout history"; "how to help a victimizer understand victimization"; and "how to educate a racist." One suggested "improved training: longer length of time to increase depth of knowledge regarding multicultural issues." Several suggestions regarding training for housing officers were related to one respondent's statement that "we need more training to teach full-time staff how to teach student staff to deal with this issue."

Comments regarding staff training included "violence: the increased number of weapons and assaults needs to be addressed" and "RAs should be better prepared to respond to an increasingly violent society and consequently student population." "Personal safety training" was recommended, and one respondent noted that "unfortunately, the time has come for staff to learn self-defense techniques." Many comments suggest a concern on the part of housing officers for the safety of staff, and comments such as "I wish I knew"; "I don't have the answers"; and "how can we help RAs to protect themselves?" suggest a need or desire to explore relevant issues further.

One issue appears to involve the expectations of RAs in confronting policy violations or disciplinary situations when it is difficult to predict in advance the potential for adverse reactions, including violence. "Confrontation training" was recommended by several persons, and one noted that "women RAs in particular need to be more assertive when harassed." Various persons suggested that staff training include "limit-setting techniques"; "how to deal with an angry person"; "skillfully handling provoked residents"; "working with upset drunk people"; "how to deal with a drunk or irrational person"; and "how to de-escalate volatile situations."

One respondent noted that confrontive communication skills should be both "effective and safe," and another emphasized that confrontation management includes "knowing when *not* to confront and seek higher help." One recommended that RAs learn to "avoid confrontations with non-students whenever possible (call for help)," and one said, "teach staff when to call for assistance so that situations don't escalate into violence." Other comments pertaining to this issue included:

- We try to teach our RAs how to defuse a situation, not heat it up. We teach mediation skills, intervention techniques and confrontation techniques and seek to impress them with the importance of regular interaction as a way of preventing future problems.
- Staff training in recognition of the various kinds of subtle to extreme victimization that occur. Combine this recognition with confrontation, communication, and position responsibilities so staff will understand their level of authority and feel comfortable about their skills.
- Ethics. A program for RAs on ethics and how it relates to the workplace will help RAs spend enough quality time on their floors and with their residents so they won't have incidents such as these occur.

Many respondents suggested that staff training involving "cultural diversity issues" or simply "learning more about other cultures" "is a must" and that it should involve an "on-going process" that "doesn't end when orientation ends." Several noted that issues affecting women, gay/lesbian students, Jewish students, and other sub-groups should be included along with those affecting racial/ethnic minority students. The following quotation illustrates the need for and potential benefit of diversity training for RAs:

- It is unlikely that a young white person, having had little personal contact or experience dealing with someone of color, will be able to feel comfortable dealing with situations where the race of the person may be viewed as a factor in the situation. Experiential training for student staff involving persons of color can help to begin the path to comfort, understanding, acceptance, and valuing with and of racial diversity.

Some respondents essentially endorsed the comment made by one that "senior administrators need to make a commitment to diversity training" and/or expressed regret that institutional commitment to diversity training is not always present. For example:

- Colleges and universities refuse to send students, faculty, staff, and administrators through cultural awareness training that in turn will help create an environment for students, faculty, staff, and administrators of color to feel more comfortable.

Additional recommendations for staff training, specifically related to harassment or other forms of victimization, ranged from initial awareness and prevention to after-the-fact discussions:

- During staff training introduce campus affirmative action officer who gives workshops on what harassment is and what procedures should be followed should it occur.

- In a following semester, without revealing personal identities, describe the incident, action, and consequences in RA training sessions.

A few respondents noted differing training needs of male and female staff, perhaps in part because it was noted that: "male students tend to be involved in perpetrating violence, vandalism, and harassment much more frequently than female students"; because there was a perceived need for "a mentor program to give young men a role model who would show them how to treat women and respect them"; or because male staff have the potential to "focus on healthy relationships with women and dispel the 'macho' image of the male college student."

It should perhaps be noted that although many college and university residence halls are coed, most floors to which individual RAs are assigned, are not. In addition, RAs are generally responsible for planning and implementing educational, cultural, social and other programs for and with students on their floors. Consequently, many of the gender-specific staff training needs were related to gender-specific student programming needs regarding men's and women's issues.

STUDENT PROGRAMMING

Many respondents recommended programming both for and about the sub-groups of students identified in this study. Although it was emphasized that programs should be ongoing, many noted that they should begin as part of orientation. Also noted was the critical nature of "the first meeting between RA and residents, the importance of establishing a good relationship, and the effects of first impressions." "At the very first floor meeting, the RA has the opportunity to project community standards and begin the community building process." "Community building is a must—the RA must have the respect of the residents."

It was suggested that the goals of "diversity programs" be to: "foster a sense of pride in one's *own* ethnic identity"; "develop a sense of understanding on campus"; "promote awareness and mutual respect for all differences"; "teach students about issues affecting others"; "educate students who may be well-meaning but are simply uninformed about people who are 'different' from themselves"; and "challenge students through programs and practice to face their value systems, their foundations, their beliefs, and how they relate to others."

It was noted that although some students are part of the problem addressed in this study, many "can be part of the solution." In order to "empower the student community so that they can help deal with [the problem]"; it was recommended that we should "not be afraid to talk about it"; that we should "bring it up as a community issue in a meeting with the living group"; and that "we must have more *dialogue* in the area of programming." "Possibly getting hall governments more involved in this area" was recommended. One example of such involvement was to "start hall watch programs (like Neighborhood Watch)." "Peer educators" were also mentioned as being particularly effective as discussion group leaders.

In addition to residence hall students, other groups of students and staff were identified as "allies" or people who can assist in programming endeavors. These include persons associated with "minority student clubs and organizations," a "multicultural affairs office," an "affirmative action office," a "campus women's center," "gay/lesbian/bisexual organizations on campus," and "a Hillel Center if your school has one; otherwise any religious leaders (I don't know of any Christian campus ministers who would not speak out against anti-Semitism)." In addition, academic courses and "pushing to get these issues into the curriculum" were discussed as means by which various issues of concern may be addressed. One respondent noted that:

- As an element in our required freshman seminar program (now in its 5th year) there is an extensive section on anti-Semitism which focuses on behaviors—I think this has helped to increase awareness on this issue.

One programming goal involves assurance that all students are made aware of campus policies. For example, recommendations included "more of an emphasis—or spreading of information—that RAs are staff of the college and are protected under the harassment policy," and "be sure sexual harassment policy is known."

It was recommended that we "engage students of all races in ethnic identity-laden projects" and noted that "education on issues affecting minority students is also critical." Other suggestions included: "more diversity training for student staff and residence hall student leaders"; "educational programs—well facilitated discussions between majority and minority students"; "make sure hall staff make an effort to connect with minority students in the hall early in the semester"; and "make every attempt to get minority students involved in hall activities and governance." In addition, the need for continual attention to programming needs was noted:

- I believe we are making positive strides in educating our resident population to the differences and subsequent respect of other cultures. We need to continue this not as a focus week but as an ongoing emphasis.

With respect to the victimization of women, respondents identified the programming needs of women, of men, and of both women and men. It was recommended that students receive "continued information regarding on-campus and off-campus safety" and noted that:

- Security systems are great, but only go so far. Women need to be educated on how to avoid situations in which they can be victimized and, equally important, men must be educated on sexual harassment and how not to be a victimizer.

It was suggested that we provide: "male issues programming"; "work with male students to better understand women's issues"; "program for male floors on the topic of rape, stereotypes, legal ramifications of any kind of victimization of women"; "give attention to interpersonal skills development and civility for male-male and male-female interactions"; discuss "relationship development and appropriate behavior"; "promote higher awareness through educational programming concerning women's issues"; "continue to raise issues regarding women's roles and rights [and] educate students on sexual harassment"; conduct "ongoing date-rape programs with males and females"; and provide "programming on sexual harassment, sexual assault, domestic violence, incest, and date rape to provide a forum for discussion" in part so that students can identify "what a friend or RA should do and what a victim can do."

Programs specifically designed for women tended to focus on issues of "empowering women" with respect to harassment and violence issues. For example, it was recommended that we "educate women on relationships, battering, rape, assertiveness, safety, etc." "Women's support groups" led by peers or staff were suggested by several respondents, one of whom noted that such groups "give women an outlet and others to relate to." In addition, it was noted that "programs for women to build self-esteem" are needed and that "alcohol/sexual issues/self-esteem types of programming can be effective in engendering personal self-actualized movement in young women."

Other programmatic suggestions regarding violence toward women involved the development of a "peer task force"; the provision of "rape whistles"; and the feeling that this is a "widespread, even though often hidden" problem that requires that residence hall staff, friends, public safety officers, and others be on "full alert."

Programming regarding "sexual preference," "sexual orientation" or "sexual minorities" was acknowledged as being difficult, particularly at institutions which do not support or condone gay/lesbian, or bisexual lifestyles. Current political and legal controversies in our larger society regarding "gay rights" were identified as reasons that some institutions or some administrators "have put the whole issue on hold" (e.g., are not actively pursuing programs on this topic). One respondent suggested that the issue of unacceptable *behaviors* (e.g., violence, vandalism, or verbal harassment) be addressed, *regardless* of the underlying constructs (e.g., personal beliefs regarding homosexuality) upon which the behaviors are based. Another noted that:

- Staff must furthermore confront their own insecurities and be educated as to dealing with incidents of victimization. The university and department must establish expectations for behavior of staff and students.

It was recommended that programs *about* gay/lesbian students be conducted not only by staff, but by "panels of gay and lesbian students" themselves. The goals of such programs were identified as including "consciousness-raising"; "promoting acceptance and understanding"; and "educating staff and students to be sensitive to these issues" so that they will "perceive these issues as serious and will offer comfort/support." Programs *for* gay/lesbian students focused on support of "gay/lesbian organizations on campus" and "founding gay/lesbian support group, if campus is without one."

It was also recommended that programs be designed to "make culture and religion more valued and widely discussed aspects of human variation"; "include religious preferences [as] religion tends to be left out of diversity programming"; "include Jewish oppression"; and "increase understanding of Jewish history and the intense hostility between certain religious and/or ethnic groups."

Several respondents noted advantages and limitations associated with making actual incidents of victimization part of our educational programming endeavors with residence hall students. The limitations, as housing officers know, are related to the issue of confidentiality regarding disciplinary matters. However, many residence hall incidents are or soon become "public information" throughout the hall or across the campus. Rumors that often follow racial incidents, for example, may be more damaging than discussing with students the actual facts of the situation and asking for student support or suggestions regarding how the situation might be resolved.

Suggestions included the following: "discuss incidents—publicize action taken when appropriate"; "use these incidents as a community learning experience"; "involve the hall community in addressing these situations"; "be willing to make an example of the situation by publicly addressing the perpetrator"; and "subject victimizers to public scrutiny, strip them of anonymity through an institutional spotlight on what they've done, and invite the community to respond."

CONFRONTING AND REPORTING INCIDENTS

Many respondents emphasized the importance of addressing and reporting (with appropriate documentation) *all* incidents, regardless of how minor they may appear to be. It was recommended that staff challenge or question even "off-handed comments" that are prejudicial, demeaning, or abusive to others; "address inappropriate use of humor which is racist in nature"; "confront the individual(s) involved"; and

- Address the problem quickly and directly. Don't allow the victimizer to hide behind other labels for racist actions. Help to educate the victimizer on what is considered "racist."

"Don't let the abuse go on" is a comment reflective of many others supporting the need to "address each incident immediately." It should be noted that concern was expressed for "protecting the victim or staff member who reported the incident." In some cases, offenders who have already demonstrated their ability and willingness to harm someone have threatened their victims with more serious harm if they report the incident. Threats to RAs if they report incidents that come to their attention were also noted. One respondent stated that:

- On each report for an incident the RA writes whether or not the person was cooperative. If uncooperative all students know this is by far one of our worst violations on campus.

Another reason cited for "treating all incidents seriously" was that "one incident perpetuates others." "All incidents of victimization should be formally reported and our staff need to make this known." Additional recommendations included: "don't ignore or cover up incidents but deal with them up front and educationally"; and "move quickly in all physical abuse situations."

ADJUDICATING INCIDENTS

With respect to the types of incidents addressed in this study, one respondent wrote, "To prevent, it probably begins with our co-curriculum: assuming self-responsibility for one's actions. To deal with, hold the student accountable." Such accountability was described in terms of "criminal prosecution," "civil action," "judicial sanctions," "punishment," "penalties," "consequences," and "education."

In reference to crimes, particularly those involving violence, it was emphasized that "perpetrators must be *prosecuted* and never have incidents watered down by a school more interested in protecting its image." It was recommended that criminal, civil, and/or disciplinary actions be "immediate," "quick," "swift," and "implemented as quickly as judicial procedures allow." Various respondents indicated that the process and/or sanctions should be "very *FIRM* but fair," "meaningful," "effective," "direct," "decisive," "appropriate to deter violations," "aggressive," "serious," "strong," "stiff," "severe," "harsh," etc. and that consequences for more serious cases should include "referral for prosecution," "encouraging civil action if appropriate," "dismissal or suspension from the institution," and "eviction from residence halls."

With respect to eviction that includes a refund of residence hall room and board fees, it was noted that this may be a desired—or even intended—outcome for students wanting to move off campus. Perhaps as a consequence, one respondent said, "Evict victimizers from housing and hold them to their rental contracts." Educational sanctions were recommended in less serious cases. Examples of comments are as follows:

- The harder the disciplinary sanction, the more the word gets out that the behavior simply won't be tolerated. I'm not speaking of eviction. Rather, give them the choice of *(a)* eviction or *(b)* a long list of educational projects and tasks to accomplish that educate them about their behavior.
- Use creative sanctions such as requiring the offending students to go on "weekend duty rounds" with an RA so they can understand what an RA must deal with on a daily basis.
- Require the offender, if known, to spend time with someone of a different ethnic background. This meeting should be supervised and documentation done by a supervisor or observer. There should be opportunities for the offender to get to know the other person.

VICTIM SERVICES

It was recommended that the "crisis intervention plan" that should be in place before a crisis occurs include descriptions of victim services. Further, it was recommended that such services involve cooperative working relationships between housing officers and resource persons both on-campus and off-campus, so that victims can receive necessary medical treatment, counseling services, legal advice, etc. as soon as possible after an incident occurs. "Having a support system available for victims" within the residence hall environment was suggested, although it was noted that "getting advice from other campus units" (e.g., multicultural affairs following a racial incident) and "working with community agencies" (e.g., a rape crisis center or shelter for battered women) are helpful or essential in some cases. It was noted that: "confidentiality is as important to the victim as it is to the accused"; and that efforts should be made to "involve the victim in the decision-making process whenever possible."

ADDITIONAL SUGGESTIONS

Additional suggestions respondents would give to other housing officers include: "try to understand behavior and why someone does this and put a plan in place"; "create smaller living units/clusters/suites if possible [in order to] lower the student to staff ratio"; have "RA duty pairs" so that no RA must confront a situation alone; provide "consistent backing and support for RAs"; "work with the RA after the incident"; "never segregate athletic teams on floor since their proportion of minorities is higher and this gives rest of the populace wrong messages and no daily contact"; and "establish an administrative office on campus to serve as a student advocate."

Although assessing the needs of and "campus climate" issues affecting *all* victim groups was suggested, the issues affecting gay/lesbian students were most frequently identified as needing such assessment. For example, one respondent said:

- Gay/lesbian/bisexual students must be included as a valid minority group on campus. In many cases their 10% is larger than any other group of difference. Research needs to drive education and policy statements.

If there is one response that briefly summarizes many or most of the suggestions respondents would make to their housing colleagues, it is the following:

- For each victim group the following are needed: clear policies, effective student orientation to them, strong staff training, strong educational programming, effective discipline process, and effective use of criminal prosecution for acts of violence.

ADDITIONAL PROFESSIONAL ISSUES

Although many professional issues have been identified in previous sections of this chapter, additional comments regarding issues to be addressed in research, conference sessions, professional publications, etc. were made. It was noted that: "we need a much better set of videos accessible to professionals in our field that deal with these topics" and that we should "share pertinent information about programs that appear to work." Topics and questions recommended for discussion among housing professionals include: "successful staff development on topics of diversity"; "mediation of concerns of *parents* of RAs who want to continue their roles"; "how to establish and provide local crisis services to residence hall students"; "how to get stu-

Suggestions and Issues Identified by Housing Officers

dents to talk with people who are different"; "greater understanding of this population [gay/lesbian students]"; "methods of helping the white students get an opportunity to feel what discrimination/harassment is like"; "how to legally respond to hate crimes"; "where does the hate originate?"; and "understanding this generation better." One respondent stated the following:

- Regarding attitudes of young men as they are leaving their high school years and entering college, it appears that a substantial number have distorted and dangerous beliefs about who women are and how they are to be viewed in society. Many of the stereotypical conservative attitudes towards women are being seen. These attitudes fly in the face of our (or any) enlightened thinking. Any further research into developing attitudes of young adult males would prove beneficial in trying to understand who our residents are.

Additional comments, regarding research needs, included: "exploration of rape culture and determining how to build safe positive environments for women"; "exploration of the 'chilly climate' for *all* women on campus"; "research on the effects of on-campus living (satisfaction, college success, etc.) for ethnic groups versus non-ethnic groups"; and "research on the relationship between RA victimization and the raising of the legal drinking age."

Chapter VII

Institutional Responses to Victimization

NO SINGLE MODEL WILL SUFFICE

The extent and the nature of violent crimes and other forms of victimization on campus may depend to varying degrees on the location of the institution (e.g., urban, suburban, rural); numbers of students enrolled; the composition of the college population (e.g., according to gender, race/ethnicity, religion, age, commuting vs. resident status); and many other factors. For example, it is not likely that the numbers and types of incidents at a two-year urban community college enrolling primarily part-time commuting adult learners would be the same as those at a large, rural, state university, where most undergraduates are traditional-age, full-time students living on campus in residence halls.

Consequently, there is no single model for responding to victimization on the college or university campus that will "fit" all institutions of higher education. Still, there appear to be some commonalities in response issues that often cross institutional boundaries. These will be discussed in this chapter.

PRIMARY, SECONDARY, AND TERTIARY RESPONSES

Institutional responses to victimization of all types may be categorized as "primary," "secondary," and "tertiary," as these terms are defined by Roark (1987, 1989) in reference to preventing violence. Essentially, primary responses are those that address environmental, attitudinal, and other conditions associated with the development of problems in the first place. Secondary responses involve identification of problems that already exist and may be growing in frequency or severity, along with programmatic and other interventions designed to resolve or mediate those problems before they erupt in violence or other serious incidents. Finally, tertiary responses involve disciplinary procedures, victim services, and other forms of intervention that are operationalized after an act of violence or another serious incident has actually occurred.

It should perhaps be emphasized at the outset that primary, secondary, and tertiary responses to violence and other problems are not options like those in a multiple choice question. Rather, *all three* must be pursued simultaneously if we wish to effectively address problems of victimization on our campuses.

RECOGNIZING THE PROBLEM AND FACTORS ASSOCIATED WITH IT

Perhaps the first step in any problem-solving process is acknowledging that a problem exists. Indeed, many college and university administrators do recognize violent crimes and other forms of victimization as problems on their campuses, and many have at least begun to implement various procedures for assessing the scope and nature of the problems on their own campuses in order to develop plans for most effectively addressing the problems. For example, a study of student affairs officers at 701 institutions affiliated with the National Association of Student Personnel Administrators (NASPA, 1991) found that:

> Most institutions have experienced significant increased concern about campus safety ... Most [respondents] said a study of campus safety is underway or was completed in the past five years ... Barely half agree that funding is adequate to ensure safety at their schools ... Four-fifths agreed that campus safety needs improvement. (p. iii)

The Anti-Defamation League of B'nai B'rith (1989) described the efforts of several organizations and agencies to assess the numbers of anti-Semitic, racist, homophobic and other "bias-motivated" incidents on college campuses and concluded that, "while these groups have calculated the total number of 'incidents' by different methods, all agree on the upward trend" (p. 1). Perhaps two of the more plausible explanations for this upward trend are as follows:

1. *The Realities of Problems Within Society*
   The attitudes and behaviors of college students tend to reflect those that are predominant in the larger society. As noted in Chapter 1, the society in question is one in which there appears to be an upward trend in violent crimes and other acts of hatred, intolerance, and bias.

2. *The Dynamics of Changing Student Populations*
   As most college and university administrators know, the student population is becoming more diverse. In particular, members of those groups that have historically been disenfranchised are growing more numerous, more visible, and more vocal on many American campuses.

Consider the impact of increased numbers of racial/ethnic minority students at historically white institutions, as described by Lomotey (1991):

Prior to the 1960s, 80 percent of African-American students attended historically black colleges. Beginning in the 1960s the trend reversed; by the end of that decade, 80% of African-American students were attending predominantly white institutions of higher education. At the same time, similar increases in enrollment at predominantly white schools occurred for Hispanics, Native Americans and Asian-Americans. (p. 264).

Lomotey (1991) explained that as diverse racial/cultural groups met and interacted on formerly all-white campuses, misunderstandings and conflicts based on "differences" that were often perceived as "disadvantages," "deficiencies," or "pathologies" erupted in both overt and covert incidents which yielded similar messages—that non-white students were not entirely welcome and that little effort would be made to accommodate their needs and address their concerns. In spite of the fact that attention to such needs and concerns has increased at many predominantly white institutions over the years, Lomotey noted that racial tensions have also increased and are expected to increase further as the college population becomes more diverse.

PUTTING VIOLENCE AND INTOLERANCE ON OUR PRIORITY LIST

In reference to racism and other forms of intolerance on campuses, Dunn (1987) offered the following insights:

How did we get into this situation, after all the progress this country has made toward putting racism behind us? The trouble is, I think, that those of us who worked in the civil-rights movement thought we had done the job ... We took racism off our priority list ... We forgot that stereotyped, racist thinking would still exist, and we didn't do enough to help our children—who hadn't lived through those years with us—to recognize and renounce its manifestations. (p. 45)

Clearly, victimization of students must be listed as a priority warranting our continual attention. However, this attention must be provided not only by housing officers, counselors, disciplinary officers, campus police, and others who deal most directly with the problem on a day-to-day basis, but by institutional leaders at the very top of the administrative hierarchy.

INVOLVING INSTITUTIONAL LEADERS

Smith (1989b) emphasized that "it is absolutely necessary that top-level administrative oversight be given to, and remain with, the campus crime problem" (p. 6). Similarly, with respect to racism in particular, Lomotey (1991) stressed that "the responsibility of college and university faculty and administrators is critical and primary. If racism is to be tackled on our campuses, the initiative must come from the top" (p. 267).

Sagaria and Koogle (1988) noted the importance of a campus alliance in empowering women. Such an alliance among various members of the college or university community is also needed if problems of victimization perpetrated against other students and staff are to be addressed in an effective manner. A steering committee is needed to coordinate the efforts of those in different sectors of the campus administration who will take different approaches to solving the problem. Clearly, multiple methods implemented by those within various departments across the campus are needed to solve multi-dimensional problems, but as most people who function within large organizations know, communication, coordination, and cooperation across departmental lines are often considerably less than ideal.

A well-coordinated institution-wide effort associated with an alliance was described by Sagaria and Koogle (1988) as "greater than the sum of its parts" (p. 89). However, these authors noted that the effectiveness of a campus alliance is enhanced if a top-level administrator who is a highly visible, respected, and influential member of the college community provides the leadership.

It may not be enough for senior administrators to appoint a committee to study the problem or to plan, implement, and evaluate strategies designed to solve the problem.

> The ultimate responsibility for responding to the campus crime problem must lie at the highest levels of campus administration. Presidents and governing boards must assure that adequate data are being gathered and analyzed to provide an accurate picture of the institution's crime risk, and must also assure that the various institutional constituencies are cooperating in the accumulation of data and in a systemic response to crime. (Smith, 1989b, p. 6)

Senior administrators may be more effective in fulfilling this responsibility if they are directly involved in the institution-wide effort to assess and address the problem. The active participation of those in high-level positions communicates very strong messages regarding how serious the administration considers the problem to be and how committed the administration is to resolving the problem. But the advantages of their involvement far exceed symbolic gestures.

For example, administrative leaders often have broad-based knowledge of many, most, or all divisions, departments, or segments of the institution. They understand existing structures, are aware of (and often have access to) financial and other resources, have power to inspire the cooperation of those in different units, and have visibility that enables them to assure many constituent groups of both personal and institutional advocacy. Their leadership often enables other committee members to accomplish more tasks in less time and certainly has the potential to yield a number and variety of positive outcomes.

Finally, the direct involvement of senior administrators in coordinating (or directly overseeing the coordination of) institution-wide efforts to address problems associated with violence and other forms of victimization on campus provides them with information and insights that they will need in order to make effective decisions and that they may be called upon to share with others, both inside and outside of the institution.

ENVIRONMENTAL ASSESSMENT AND LONG-TERM PLANNING

Campus climates or student perceptions of campus environments differ not only from one institution to another, but also from one group to another on the same campus. Assessing our environments and their impacts on the college experience of various subgroups of students is an important first step in developing long-term plans to improve the quality of education provided to all students. The Anti-Defamation League of B'nai B'rith (1989) emphasized three major tasks inherent in "making the campus a better place:"

> The campus environment needs to be carefully and continually scrutinized. The campus environment can contribute to a positive multicultural learning experience or it can produce tension and polarization. Campus officials must begin an ongoing process of institutional self-examination and rectification that involves all segments of the campus community ...
>
> Faculty and administrators must establish high priority long-term human relations programming within the curriculum, in the orientation process, through the student services and in university publications. We must all work to build for the future as well as fight the fires that emerge from time to time ...
>
> Administrators and faculty have an ongoing responsibility to speak out on matters that could create or affect tensions on campus so as to ameliorate conflict and put the institution on public record. (p. 13)

EDUCATING STUDENTS AND STAFF

Libraries, professional journals, conference programs, etc. offer an abundance of information concerning the education of college students, both within and outside of the formal classroom. Clearly, the literature concerning human relations training; multicultural programs and courses; racism workshops; security awareness efforts; rape prevention programs; seminars concerning issues faced by gay, lesbian, or bisexual students; residence hall staff training; and the many other types of educational endeavors directly or indirectly to the topic of victimization are beyond the scope of this book. However, three major points concerning educational programming will be addressed.

Recognize That One Program Is Never Enough

Like our overall response to victimization, a specific response in the form of a single educational program may not "fit" all students in all situations. For example, Lenihan, Rawlins, Eberly, Buckley, and Masters (1992) summarized the effects of a date rape education program on the attitudes of 821 university students. Their study found that, although women's attitudes changed substantially following this intervention, men were generally resistant to the program and adhered to their previous attitudes and beliefs in various myths concerning rape.

It seems clear that different types of intervention are needed to address different issues with different groups of students at different times. Thus, our programming efforts should be ongoing throughout the year and should use multiple methods, including both traditional approaches (e.g., lectures, films/videos, panel discussions) and theatrical, peer advocate, and other creative approaches.

Maximize the Use of "Teachable Moments"

For both legal and ethical reasons, confidentiality associated with disciplinary incidents must be maintained. However, some of the public or quasi-public incidents of victimization should be identified as presenting what educators generally refer to as "teachable moments." Just as most people become more security conscious (at least for awhile) immediately following news reports of a crime in their own neighborhood, students tend to be most receptive to educational programs concerning victimization when it comes to their attention that an incident has actually occurred within their own community.

One example of taking advantage of a "teachable moment" was provided by Avasthi (1990), who described several interventions designed to educate students and give students an opportunity to discuss racism and its impact on their community immediately after the initials "KKK" were found carved into the wall of a residence hall bathroom. Dunn (1987) reported that, after a college newspaper printed letters concerning difficulties minority group members encountered in residential life, the following was found painted on the steps of the administration building: "Niggers, Spics, and Chinks, quit complaining or get out" (p. 44). Dunn, president of the college, indicated that she immediately called an all-campus meeting during which students, faculty members and administrators "aired our responses to the incident and talked about what we could do, personally and administratively, to insure that nothing like this would occur in the future" (p. 44).

Never Underestimate the Power of the Peer Group

Although it is doubtful that those who have worked with college students for any length of time would underestimate the power of the peer group in general, it should be noted that the power of peers in promoting understanding and appreciation of "differences" on our campuses is only beginning to be explored. Dalton (1991) observed that "peer culture and peer leaders, which exert the most influence on the values and behaviors of college students, can be obstacles in educators' efforts to eliminate bias and promote tolerance, or they can be powerful allies in these endeavors" (p. 1). His book, described further in Chapter VIII, focuses on strategies for encouraging students to be allies in providing peer intervention programs, challenging expressions of bias or intolerance in the peer group, combatting harassment and other incidents, etc.

Although some of the "most common" and "most serious" incidents described in Chapter V were apparently perpetrated by non-students or at least persons not known to be students, most seem to have been perpetrated by the institution's very own students. Administrators must resist temptations to blame members of the off-campus community for the campus crime problem, and acknowledge that students are most often victimized by other students, often other residents of their own hall, floor, and even room. While it was most clear in the descriptions of incidents victimizing resident assistants and women, it is hypothesized that other students are similarly victimized by people they know or at least pass by every day in the hallway, in the stairwells, in the dining room, etc. of their residence hall—a place that should offer them welcome, acceptance, security, etc. as their campus "home."

It is not likely that college officials can solve the problem of victimization on campus by themselves (i.e., without the help of the students). Clearly, some students are a part of the "problem" addressed in this study, but other students (perhaps the overwhelming majority) can be a part of the "solution." Most housing officers are familiar with the havoc that can be created by *one* student in a residence hall housing 500 students. Indeed, perhaps our greatest challenge is creating ways to empower the many to educate, deter, confront, and/or report the few who would, for example, spray paint a swastika in the elevator, yell racist epithets from a window, shred the clothing of a lesbian woman, rape or otherwise assault a woman, or threaten to harm or kill an RA.

Students, the vast majority of whom most likely abhor the sight of a swastika in the elevator, or cringe when they hear racist epithets yelled from windows, etc., need to know that we need and want their help in preventing these and other acts of victimization.

EXERCISING OUR OWN FIRST AMENDMENT RIGHTS

Both of the examples in the previous section involve not only hate speech, but vandalism in the form of damage to institutional property. Thus, the perpetrators of the incidents, if they could be identified, should be subject to institutional discipline and criminal prosecution. However, incidents of hateful or offensive speech that involve no violations of laws or institutional policies often frustrate and bewilder college officials.

> Coast to coast, it seems, racial tensions on American university campuses have been rising for several years. Increasingly rough words are being spoken, lines defiantly drawn. And the schools themselves are in an exquisite dilemma, forced to defend by turns the principle of free speech that, more than anything else, defines the spirit of

truth-seeking for which universities are said to stand, and the right of their students—especially those who are members of racial and other minorities—to seek the truth in surroundings free of hatred and intimidation. (France, 1990, p. 44)

Policies restricting speech based solely on the content of such speech would most likely be found unconstitutional in public colleges and universities. However, college officials are not without power to respond to speech that is degrading and humiliating, demeans the dignity of others, promotes feelings of intimidation or fear, or otherwise hurts people. After all, administrators and faculty are citizens, too, and they can use their own first amendment rights to speak out in personal opposition to words of hatred or intolerance that inflict injury on others.

College officials must be sensitive to the harmful and often silencing effects that hate speech has on its victims in order to challenge the not uncommon belief that victims "overreact" to expressions of hatred that remain at the verbal (oral or written) level. For example, Cole (1991) indicated that the defacement of posters, one of which had the term "niggers" written on it, had led to considerable distress, anger, and tears on the part of some students in a campus residence hall and that some other students were then "heard to wonder what the big deal was" (p. 226).

A group of residential administrators asked these and other students to "pause to wonder at the term 'over-reaction,' and consider what causes someone to judge and try to invalidate the feelings of another person. How can we assess someone else's pain or grief? How can we calibrate it and decide what is just the right amount of anguish for that person to feel? On the other hand, how do we find the courage it takes to hear, accept and even empathize with another's suffering?" (Cole, 1991, p. 226)

Indeed, administrators are called upon not only to hear, accept and empathize with the suffering incurred by the victims of hate speech, but also to respond by providing support to victims and by personally speaking out in opposition to incidents of intolerance and oppression.

UNDERSTANDING THE CONSEQUENCES OF VICTIMIZATION

As readers may recall, a few of the items at the beginning of the survey form referred to full-time residence hall staff. However, the victimization of such staff was not assessed in this study. Consequently, some of the findings from another study will be used in this section to describe not only the victimization of professional staff, but the consequences of such victimization.

The study in question was conducted by William H. Parsonage, professor in the Department of Administration of Justice at The Pennsylvania State University, and the students enrolled in his spring semester, 1992 course entitled "Perspectives on Victimization." The study involved an extensive survey, completed by 227 RAs and coordinators (full-time, ten-month, professional staff), and was summarized in a research report entitled, *The Victimization of Pennsylvania State University Resident Assistants and Coordinators in the Line of Duty* (Parsonage et al., 1992). (Please note that this report is described further in Chapter VIII.)

One portion of the survey form asked respondents to describe and to answer several questions concerning "the SINGLE MOST SERIOUS victimizing incident against you in your role as an RA or Coordinator DURING YOUR CAREER." Twenty-three (82%) of the 28 coordinators did so. Very briefly, it should be noted that the perpetrators of these "single most serious" incidents victimizing coordinators were most likely to be students for whom the coordinators were responsible (65%) or other residence hall students (17%) and that the incidents themselves were most likely to involve threat of harm (26%); other verbal harassment (17%); and physical assault, harassing language, and other public harassment (13%) each.

One set of items concerned the consequences of these "single most serious" incidents. More than half of the coordinators who described such incidents indicated that they had experienced anger (91%); no physical injury, but shaken up (82%); reduced trust in residence hall students (70%); anxiety (70%); helplessness (65%); rehashed event over and over (65%); disruption to personal life (65%); stomachache, headache, similar problems (57%); body tension (57%); difficulty falling asleep (52%); avoid contact with threatening students (52%); concern that job causes victimization (52%); and thought about resigning (52%).

Between one-third and one-half reported reduced self confidence (48%); reduced sensitivity to residence hall students (48%); increased irritability (48%); sadness (44%); fear on the job (39%); awakening at night (39%); and depression (35%). In addition, consequences experienced by fewer than one-third of these coordinators included physical injuries, nausea, loss of appetite, nightmares related to the incident, inability to reconcile the incident, withdrawal from activities, avoiding contact with other staff, negative change in relationship with coworkers, etc.

Most housing officers who do have or have had live-in positions in residence halls would probably acknowledge that the victimization of staff and the consequences of such victimization are no worse at The Pennsylvania State University than they are at many or most other institutions of higher education. Clearly, such acts of victimization may (at least temporarily) disrupt the personal lives of staff and interfere with their ability to most effectively do their jobs.

Similar personal consequences may affect the lives of students who are victimized by violence, vandalism, and verbal harassment. In addition, students (including student RAs) may experience academic consequences in terms of obtaining lower grades, dropping courses, or withdrawing from school. For example, it is not uncommon for minority students to withdraw from school following racial incidents or for women students to withdraw as a consequence of having been raped.

PROVIDING SERVICES TO VICTIMS AND OFFENDERS

The need for a campus or community rape advocate service cannot be overstated. Immediately following rapes and other violent crimes, victims experience emotional turmoil that makes clear, rational decision-making very difficult. Nevertheless, decisions regarding medical examinations involving protocols for the collection of evidence, medical tests for pregnancy and sexually transmitted diseases, medical treatment for physical injuries sustained, the notification of police, and the pressing of criminal or civil charges, should be made as soon after the assault as possible.

Rape advocates should be highly trained to offer emotional support to victims while informing them of their rights and options and assisting them in making decisions. "Rape survivors have stated time and again that rape crisis advocates have been most helpful in their ability to deal with the assault. Twice as helpful as physicians and three times more helpful than the police" (Glidden, 1992, p. 8).

Perhaps rape advocate services or services provided to women involved in violent relationships could serve as models for the development of similar advocacy services for those who have been victimized by other types of offenses. Indeed, a common concern is that the criminal justice system generally provides perpetrators with information regarding how the system works, offers legal counsel, and follows specific procedures in order to ensure that "due process" and other rights of the accused are protected without providing similar information and services to protect the rights of victims.

Assuming that victims have not been physically injured and do not need immediate medical attention, perhaps their primary need following an incident is the need for information concerning various actions they might take. What can they do now? Whom can they call? What will happen if they report the incident to college officials or police? What legal assistance is available to them? What counseling services or victim support groups are available? It should perhaps be noted that the Student Right-to-Know and Campus Security Act (20 U.S.C. 1092), including recently incorporated sections concerning the rights of sexual assault victims, requires that the answers to many of these and other questions be provided to the victims of various crimes.

Administrators should understand that the indecision, often yielding inaction, on the part of many victims is based on fear that whatever they do will only make matters worse for them. Such fear (e.g., that perpetrators will harm them further, peers will turn against them, or parents will withdraw them from school if they tell others about the incident) should be discussed within the context of a given student's own particular situation, taking into consideration the realities of the services that can be provided to assist students who choose different methods of addressing their victimization.

Every campus should have one or more persons designated to receive calls from students who believe they have been victimized in any way and to provide information and guidance to such students. When incidents involving hate speech, offensive comments, general harassment, or vandalism either have unknown perpetrators or do not involve crimes or violations of institutional policies, it is important that students receive advice or direction regarding constructive methods of expressing their grievances by letting others know how angry or offended or hurt they feel. Such students should also be asked for their suggestions regarding what they believe the institution or any part of the institution (including student groups) can and should do to address their grievances.

Finally, institutions must address the needs of the perpetrators of the types of incidents addressed in this study. Some perpetrators may need medical attention, some may need legal assistance, many may need information regarding the workings of the institution's disciplinary system, and many (perhaps most) may need (or be able to benefit from) professional counseling.

In some cases, perpetrators are not identified and specific victims do not step forward to register complaints. For example, consider racist, anti-Semitic, homophobic, sexually offensive, or other graffiti appearing in elevators or on sidewalks, walls, doors, bulletin boards, etc. Most agree that such graffiti should be removed as soon as possible, but if this is the standard and the *only* response, college officials may be perceived as abrogating their responsibilities to make any attempt to identify perpetrators, acknowledge the pain that the graffiti may have inflicted on people, speak out in condemning such acts of victimization, discuss the costs of such vandalism throughout the campus community, identify underlying attitudes expressed in the graffiti, and develop strategies for minimizing the reoccurrence of such incidents.

BUILDING BRIDGES BETWEEN THE INSTITUTION'S DISCIPLINARY SYSTEM AND SOCIETY'S CRIMINAL JUSTICE SYSTEM

It is essential that college officials maintain positive working relationships with those associated with law enforcement agencies (both on and off campus) and those associated with the criminal and civil court systems within the community. When appropriate, incidents occurring in residence halls specifically, or on the campus more generally, should be reported to law enforcement officials and, in some cases, may be referred for civil action.

Student conduct codes vary from one institution to another, depending on institutional missions, institutional values, student and campus realities, and many other factors. Historically, institutions have differed according to the extent to which the courts have been used to adjudicate incidents occurring on campus. Some administrators have preferred to deal with almost all student incidents "internally." Others have argued that if we are truly concerned about the development of students as adults who are accountable for their own behaviors, we may be giving students the "wrong messages" by allowing them to face only institutional disciplinary sanctions for actions that are indeed defined as "crimes" within our society, and that if committed off-campus, would be subject to criminal prosecution.

Recent federal laws, particularly the Student Right-to-Know and Campus Security Act (20 *U.S.C.* 1092) and the Drug-Free Schools and Communities Act Amendments of 1989 (20 *U.S.C.* 3224a, with regulations at 34 *C.F.R.* 86), have clarified the legal duties of college officials with respect to notifying law enforcement officers when various crimes are committed on campus. It is incumbent on all administrators to educate themselves and members of their staff in reference to these and other duties as defined by law.

All housing officers are referred in Chapter VIII to the recently revised edition of *Administering College and University Housing: A Legal Perspective* (Gehring, 1992) for an introduction to legal issues associated with their work. However, it is emphasized that neither one's reading of books nor one's own direct reading of laws themselves can substitute for ongoing consultation with one's own institutional legal counsel.

SUMMARY

No single model for addressing problems of violence and other forms of victimization on campus will "fit" the very diverse systems of higher education within the United States. Rather, officials at all institutions must acknowledge and assess the extent and nature of problems on their own campuses and develop strategies to create campus climates that are not conducive to victimization, resolve conflicts as they are developing so that they will not result in victimization, and most effectively address incidents of victimization that do occur.

Campus violence and other incidents that victimize students and staff must be considered priority items and must be addressed by those at the very top of the campus administration. These college officials must coordinate a multi-dimensional and campus-wide effort to address issues of victimization and provide both the leadership and the resources for activities ranging from assessment of current conditions within the campus environment to long-term planning that will create a campus environment in which civility, acceptance, and respect for individual differences will predominate in the future.

Extensive efforts must be made to educate faculty, staff, and students so that they will be not only better informed of the issues related to problems of victimization on campus, but empowered to help solve those problems. Administrators must take advantage of every opportunity to make good use of "teachable moments" when incidents occur and be willing to exercise their own rights to free speech by making it clear that they do not condone acts of violence, vandalism, or verbal harassment that inflict injury on any member(s) of the college or university community.

College officials must acknowledge that personal, academic, and (in the case of staff) professional consequences of victimization are extensive. Further, they must provide the necessary support, counseling, medical, legal, and other services needed by both victims and perpetrators. If such services are not available and cannot be made available on the campus, effective referrals to equivalent services within the community must be made.

Finally, college officials must be informed of their legal duties, maintain positive working relationships with law enforcement officials, make necessary referrals for criminal prosecution or civil action, and consult regularly with institutional legal counsel.

Only by taking action to create campus climates wherein civility and respect for the rights of others predominate, by effectively addressing issues or concerns before they become serious problems, and by responding appropriately to acts of violence and other forms of victimization can college officials provide reasonably safe and secure environments for students, staff, and faculty.

Chapter VIII

Recommended Resources

All resources cited in this book are listed in the reference section following this chapter. Many references focus on issues related to violence and other forms of victimization very broadly, while others focus on such issues as they affect college campuses in particular. Still others deal with such issues as they relate specifically to what occurs in college and university residence halls. Several resources judged to be particularly worthy of the attention of housing officers, residential life professionals, and other college and university administrators are described briefly in this chapter.

. . . .

Parsonage, W., Barbiero, M., Bartoo, K., Febbraro, A., Hoffman, R., Ichter, L., Lawrence, T., Rivera, S., Sculimbrene, P., Terry, E., Traub, M., & Wernovsky, H. (1992). *The victimization of Pennsylvania State University resident assistants and coordinators in the line of duty: A research report.* University Park, PA: The Pennsylvania State University, Department of Administration of Justice.

Only a small portion of the information contained in this research report (i.e., the portion concerning the consequences of victimization as experienced by coordinators) was summarized in Chapter VII. However, it is recommended that housing officers who are concerned about the victimization of staff review the entire report, as it summarizes a study that involved the following ten research questions:

1. How extensive is the victimization of Penn State resident assistants and coordinators in the line of duty?
2. Do the kinds and rates of victimizations vary according to the specific roles of workers?
3. What kinds of victimizations occur?

4. Does victimization experience vary by worker characteristics [e.g., gender, race]?
5. Who victimizes resident assistants and coordinators?
6. In what context do victimizations occur?
7. How do resident assistants and coordinators deal with these events?
8. What are the aftermaths of victimizations?
9. How much victimization of workers can be prevented?
10. To what extent do resident assistants and coordinators endorse various proposed policy initiatives as having the potential to reduce victimization? (p. 21)

For additional information, contact Professor William H. Parsonage, Department of Administration of Justice, 1001 Oswald Tower, The Pennsylvania State University, State College, PA.

. . . .

National Association of Student Personnel Administrators, Research and Program Development Division. (1991). *Campus safety: A survey of administrative perceptions and strategies.* Washington, DC: Author.

This report summarizes the responses to the "Campus Safety Questionnaire," completed by 701 chief student affairs officers, representing two-thirds of all NASPA member institutions.

The questionnaire was designed to collect data on general perceptions of campus safety, management structure, crime reporting practices, and campus safety features and services. The survey also asked about in-house safety studies pending or completed, state legislation, adequacy of safety funding, and sense of institutional concern. Finally, the questionnaire asked for a short description of campus safety programs or initiatives deemed successful. (p. 2)

The successful programs and initiatives were sorted into five categories including "traditional services" (e.g., campus police/campus security, crime prevention or response services, student-staffed security programs); "environmental and technological modifications" (e.g., landscaping, lighting, security telephones and cameras, computers, card access); "planning, policy, and information strategies" (e.g., using crime reports, safety studies and other information "to guide administrative decision making and to enhance campus awareness"); "education and support programs" (e.g., security awareness programs, victim advocacy and support services); and "community action" (e.g., involving those on campus and in the surrounding community in activities that will enhance safety) (p. v).

Of particular interest to housing officers may be general ratings of safety in residence halls and responses to nine items regarding safety features in residence halls. For additional information, contact the

NASPA Central Office, 1875 Connecticut Avenue NW, Suite 418, Washington, DC 20009-5728.

. . . .

Sherrill, J. M., & Siegel, D. G. (Eds.). (1989). *Responding to violence on campus* (New Directions for Student Services No. 47). San Francisco: Jossey-Bass.

The eight chapters in this book focus on the history of violence on campus, research on campus violence, violence in residence halls (including courtship violence), acquaintance rape and other forms of sexual violence, counseling victims and perpetrators, legal issues, various models used in responding to campus violence, and additional sources of information. Readers interested in the assessment of campus violence may be particularly interested in reviewing copies of two survey forms provided in the appendix. To order this book, write to Jossey-Bass Publishers, Inc., 350 Sansome Street, San Francisco, CA 94104.

. . . .

Reynolds, A. L., & von Destinon, M. (date unspecified). *Campus violence manual.* Washington, DC: American College Personnel Association, Campus Violence Project.

The information in this 102-page manual was compiled by members of the Campus Violence Project Task Force, affiliated with the American College Personnel Association (ACPA). Manuals were (and continue to be) distributed to participants in workshops on campus violence that were (and continue to be) sponsored by ACPA and offered at various locations throughout the United States.

Various sections of the manual (most of them used, discussed, or referred to during the workshop) focus on definitions, an institutional planning model, useful assessment tools, case studies, legal issues, and violence treatment programs. One section provides ten short articles concerning campus violence issues. The final section, written by Dr. Mary L. Roark, is entitled "Annotated Bibliography for Preventing Campus Violence" and contains brief descriptions of more than 200 books, articles, reports, videotapes, and organizations focusing on campus crime, bias-related violence, courtship violence, rape and sexual assault, crisis intervention, mediation and judicial issues, and other topics related to violence on campus.

For further information concerning ACPA's workshops on campus violence and the accompanying manual, contact the American College Personnel Association, 1 Dupont Circle, Suite 360A, Washington, DC 20036-1110.

. . . .

American College Personnel Association. (1992). *Campus violence redefined: A teleconference for campus leaders (Participant's Guide).* Washington, DC: Author.

Recommended Resources

This manual was distributed to those who attended viewings of the April 8, 1992 live broadcast of the interactive teleconference entitled "Campus Violence Redefined: A Teleconference for Campus Leaders," sponsored by the American College Personnel Association (ACPA) and the National University Teleconference Network (NUTN). The two-hour telecast included segments focusing on definitions, demographics, and statistics; prevention efforts; and institutional responses. The "Participant's Guide" contains sections concerning definitions, factors underlying campus violence, preventing campus violence, case studies, and resources. For further information concerning the teleconference video and manual, contact the American College Personnel Association, 1 Dupont Circle, Suite 360A, Washington, DC 20036-1110.

. . . .

Smith, M. C. (1989). *Crime and campus police: A handbook for police officers and administrators.* Asheville, NC: College Administration Publications, Inc.

This book addresses topics of concern not only to campus police, but to other college officials as well. They include administrator responsibilities, violence on campus, criminal procedures, campus judicial procedures, civil and criminal liability, and consequences for the institution, along with many other topics related to crime on campus. To order a copy of the book, contact College Administration Publications, Inc., P.O. Box 15898, Asheville, NC 28813-0898.

. . . .

Gehring, D. D. (Ed.). (1992). *Administering college and university housing: A legal perspective.* Asheville, NC: College Administration Publications, Inc.

First published in 1983, this book has recently been revised to include updated information. Given not only issues related to the victimization of students in residence halls, but the many more legal issues affecting the housing profession today, it is recommended that this book be placed on the "absolutely must read" list of every housing administrator.

This book includes chapters entitled, "Legal information: A part of the decision making process," "Constitutional issues in the residence halls," "Statutes and regulations affecting residence hall operations and staff," "Contracts and their use in housing," "Torts: Your legal duties and responsibilities," "The privileges and responsibilities of tax exempt status," and "Managing the risk." This revised edition also includes information concerning the Student Right-to-Know and Campus Security Act, the Drug-Free Schools and Communities Act, the Americans with Disabilities Act, and other recent legislation and litigation that affect the administration of college and university housing.

This book is available from College Administration Publications, Inc., P.O. Box 15898, Asheville, NC 28813-0898.

Pavela, G. (Ed.). *Synthesis: Law and Policy in Higher Education.* Asheville, NC: College Administration Publications, Inc.

Each edition of this periodical, published four times annually, focuses on legal issues and policy implications related to a specific topic of concern to higher education (e.g., crime on campus, acquaintance rape on campus, etc.). In addition, readers may wish to note that "sister publications," the *Synfax Weekly Report* and the *Synfax Bulletin,* are sent to subscribers via telefax on a weekly and immediate need-to-know basis, respectively. For example, recent *Synfax Bulletins* have addressed campus response to the Rodney King verdict and a United States Supreme Court decision and Congressional hearing that have implications for campus "hate speech" policies.

For additional information concerning *Synthesis: Law and Policy in Higher Education,* contact College Administration Publications, Inc., P.O. Box 15898, Asheville, NC 28813-0898. For additional information concerning the *Synfax Weekly Report* and *Synfax Bulletin,* call (800) 995-SFAX or write to Synfax, 1882 Harcourt Avenue, Crofton, MD 21114.

Gehring, D. D., & Geraci, C. P. (1989). *Alcohol on campus: A compendium of the law and a guide to campus policy* and Gehring, D. D. (1991). *1990 update to alcohol on campus: A compendium of the law and a guide to campus policy.* Asheville, NC: College Administration Publications, Inc.

The 1989 edition of this book contains chapters entitled "The developing public policy," "Alcohol on campus," "Sources of liability," "Developing alcohol policies and risk management procedures," and "State annotations." The "State annotations" chapter provides brief reviews of statutory and case law related to alcohol on campus in each of the fifty states and the District of Columbia. These reviews concern "definition of a minor," "possession or consumption by a minor," "sale or gift to a minor," "misrepresentation of age," "sale or gift to an intoxicated person," "definition of intoxicated persons," "dramshop liability," "social host liability," and "other cases of interest." Appendices include "Resolution of National Inter-Fraternity Council," "Inter-Association Guidelines for Beverage/Alcohol Marketing on College and University Campuses," "Inter-Association Model Campus Alcohol Policy," "Collegiate Alcohol Risk Assessment Guide," and "An Introduction to Legal Research."

The *1990 Update* summarizes changes in statutes and case law that occurred since the original volume was published. In addition, it provides cumulative updated tables summarizing dramshop liability and social host liability in each of the fifty states and the District of Columbia. Both volumes are available from College Administration Publications, Inc., P.O. Box 15898, Asheville, NC 28813-0898.

Olivas, M. A. (Special Issue Ed.), & Silverman, R. J. (Ed.). (1992, September/October). *The Journal of Higher Education (Special Issue—Racial Harassment on Campus), 63*(5).

This special issue contains articles entitled, "Civil rights vs. civil liberties: The case of discriminatory verbal harassment" by T. C. Grey, "A proposed process for managing the First Amendment aspects of campus hate speech" by W. A. Kaplin, "The campus racial climate: Contexts for conflict" by S. Hurtado, and "The political economy of immigration, intellectual property, and racial harassment: Case studies of the implementation of legal change on campus" by M. A. Olivas. In addition, Olivas provides an extensive bibliography on racial harassment/hate speech. *The Journal of Higher Education* is published bimonthly in affiliation with the American Association for Higher Education by The Ohio State University Press, 1070 Carmack Road, Columbus, OH 43210.

Dalton, J. C. (1991). *Racism on campus: Confronting racial bias through peer interventions* (New Directions for Student Services No. 56). San Francisco: Jossey-Bass.

This book is recommended for several reasons. First, it describes campus diversity, racial identity, racial consciousness, gay/lesbian/bisexual identity, and other specific models that can help us to identify stages in which our institutions and students find themselves. Second, it outlines specific types of programmatic and other interventions that are most effective at specific stages of development.

Third, this book provides sample role plays, handouts, exercises, workshop designs, etc. that would be useful in programming for residence hall students. And fourth, the information contained in this book may be particularly useful in developing staff training programs for that group of "peer leaders" known as Resident Assistants (RAs). The book is available from Jossey-Bass Publishers, Inc., 350 Sansome Street, San Francisco, CA 94104-1310.

The Journal of College and University Student Housing, The ACUHO-I Talking Stick, and other publications of the Association of College and University Housing Officers-International.

Resources dealing most specifically with issues of concern to housing officers are those published by the Association of College and University Housing Officers-International (ACUHO-I). Issues involving violence and other forms of victimization in residence halls, along with implications for policy making, staff training, student programming, etc., are discussed often in these publications.

For example, a partial listing of topics explored in *The Journal of College and University Student Housing* and *The ACUHO-I Talking Stick* include vandalism in residence halls (Bowles, 1982), regulations for hate speech in residence halls (Janosik, 1991; Palmer, 1991), multicultural training programs for residence hall staff (Grubbs, 1985), crime prevention in residence halls (Smith, 1990), residence hall discipline systems (Pitts & Waryold, 1990), legal liability related to student safety (Gibbs, 1989; Hulm, 1990), and assisting rape victims in residence halls (Palmer, 1992).

For additional information concerning these publications, contact the ACUHO-I Central Support Services Office, 101 Curl Drive, Suite 140, Columbus, OH 43210-1195.

References

The ACUHO-I Talking Stick. Columbus, OH: Association of College and University Housing Officers–International

The American College Personnel Association. (1992). *Campus violence redefined: A teleconference for campus leaders (Participant's Guide).* Washington, DC: Author.

The Anti-Defamation League of B'nai B'rith. (1989). *Combatting bigotry on campus.* New York: Author.

Astin, A. (1982). *Minorities in American higher education: Recent trends, current prospects and recommendations.* San Francisco: Jossey-Bass Publishers.

Avasthi, S. (1990). Residence hall challenges intensify. *Guidepost, 33*(5), 1, 5.

Barr, M. J. (1989). Legal issues confronting student affairs practice. In U. Delworth, G. R. Hanson & Associates (Eds.), *Student Services: A handbook for the profession,* second edition (pp. 80-111). San Francisco: Jossey-Bass Publishers.

Bogal-Allbritten, R. B., & Allbritten, W. L. (1989). The hidden victims: Courtship violence among college students. *Journal of College Student Personnel, 26*(3), 201-204.

Bowles, J. K. (1982). The residence hall vandalism problem: A model for examining destructive behavior. *Journal of College and University Student Housing, 12*(1), 15-19.

Cerio, N. G. (1989). Counseling victims and perpetrators of campus violence. In J. M. Sherrill & D. G. Siegel (Eds.), *Responding to violence on campus* (New Directions for Student Services No. 47., pp. 53-63). San Francisco: Jossey-Bass Publishers.

Cockey, M., Sherrill, J. M., & Cave, R. B. II. (1989). Towson State University's research on campus violence. In J. M. Sherrill & D. G. Siegel (Eds.), *Responding to violence on campus* (New Directions for Student Services No. 47, pp. 17-27). San Francisco: Jossey-Bass Publishers.

Cole, S. (1991). Beyond recruitment and retention: The Stanford experience. In P. G. Altbach & K. Lomotey (Eds.), *The racial crisis in American higher education* (pp. 213-232). Albany, NY: State University of New York Press.

Cowley, W. H. (1934). The history of residential student housing. *School and Society, 40,* 705-712, 758-764.

Dalton, J. C. (Ed.). (1991). *Racism on campus: Confronting racial bias through peer interventions* (New Directions for Student Services No. 56). San Francisco: Jossey-Bass Publishers.

Dunn, M. M. (1987, April 29). Intolerance on campuses: We took racism off our priority list. *The Chronicle of Higher Education,* 44-45.

Durant, C. E., Marston, L. L., & Eisenhandler, S. (1986). *Findings from the 1985 national RA harassment survey: Frequency and types of RA harassment and ways to deal with the problem.* Amherst, MA: University of Massachusetts, Division of Housing Services.

FBI: Violent crime by youth up 25% in decade. (1992, August 30). *The Columbus Dispatch,* p. 1.

Fleming, J. (1984). *Blacks in college.* San Francisco: Jossey-Bass Publishers.

France, S. (1990, July). Hate goes to college. *ABA Journal, 44,* 46, 48-49.

Gehring, D. D. (Ed.). (1992). *Administering college and university housing: A legal perspective.* Asheville, NC: College Administration Publications, Inc.

Gehring, D. D. (1991). *1990 update to alcohol on campus: A compendium of the law and a guide to campus policy.* Asheville, NC: College Administration Publications, Inc.

Gehring, D. D., & Geraci, C. P. (1989). *Alcohol on campus: A compendium of the law and a guide to campus policy.* Asheville, NC: College Administration Publications, Inc.

Gibbs, A. (1989). Concerns regarding legal liability for student safety. *Journal of College and University Student Housing, 19*(2), 3-5.

Glidden, M. V. (1992, April). Women fight back: Taking action against rape. *National NOW Times, 8,* 10.

Grubbs, L. L. (1985). Multicultural training in university residence halls. *Journal of College and University Student Housing, 15*(2), 21-25.

Hulm, T. T. (1990). The (un)safe campus and university liability. *Journal of College and University Student Housing, 20*(2), 7-11.

In brief. (1987a, May 20). *The Chronicle of Higher Education,* p. 2.

In brief. (1987b, June 24). *The Chronicle of Higher Education,* p. 2.

Janosik, S. (1991). Additional regulations for hate speech in residence halls? No. *Journal of College and University Student Housing, 21*(2), 25-26.

The Journal of College and University Student Housing. Columbus, OH: Association of College and University Housing Officers–International

Lenihan, G. O., Rawlins, M. E., Eberly, C. G., Buckley, B., & Masters, B. (1992). Gender differences in rape supportive attitudes before and after a date rape education intervention. *Journal of College Student Development, 33*(4), 331-338.

Lomotey, K. (1991). Conclusion. In P. G. Altbach & K. Lomotey (Eds.), *The racial crisis in American higher education* (pp. 263-268). Albany, NY: State University of New York Press.

Marable, M. (1988, September/October). The beast is back: An analysis of campus racism. *The Black Collegian*, 52-54.

National Association of Student Personnel Administrators, Research and Program Development Division. (1991). *Campus safety: A survey of administrative perceptions and strategies.* Washington, DC: Author.

Olivas, M. A. (Special Issue Ed.) & Silverman, R. J. (Ed.). (1992, September/October). *The Journal of Higher Education (Special Issue— Racial Harassment on Campus), 63*(5).

Palmer, C. J. (1991). Additional regulations for hate speech in residence halls? Yes. *Journal of College and University Student Housing, 21*(2), 27-30.

Palmer, C. J. (1992). The aftermath of rape: Strategies for assisting victims. *ACUHO-I Talking Stick, 9*(6), 8-9.

Parsonage, W., Barbiero, M., Bartoo, K., Febbraro, A., Hoffman, R., Ichter, L., Lawrence, T., Rivera, S., Sculimbrene, P., Terry, E., Traub, M., & Wernovsky, H. (1992). *The victimization of Pennsylvania State University resident assistants and coordinators in the line of duty: A research report.* State College, PA: The Pennsylvania State University, Department of Administration of Justice.

Pitts, J. H., & Waryold, D. (1990). Conducting a sanction enhancement group as an alternative to punishment in a university residence hall discipline system. *Journal of College and University Student Housing, 20*(1), 18-20.

Rickgarn, R. L. V. (1989). Violence in residence halls: Campus domestic violence. In J. M. Sherrill & D. G. Siegel (Eds.), *Responding to violence on campus* (New Directions for Student Services No. 47, pp. 29-40). San Francisco: Jossey-Bass Publishers.

Roark, M. L. (1987). Preventing violence on college campuses. *Journal of Counseling and Development, 65*(7), 367-371.

Roark, M. L. (1989). Sexual violence. In J. M. Sherrill & D. G. Siegel (Eds.), *Responding to violence on campus* (New Directions for Student Services No. 47, pp. 41-52). San Francisco: Jossey-Bass Publishers.

Sagaria, M. D., & Koogle, L. L. (1988). Greater than the sum of its parts: Strategy and resources. In M. D. Sagaria (Ed.), *Empowering women: Leadership development strategies on campus* (New Directions for Student Services No. 44, pp. 89-103). San Francisco: Jossey-Bass Publishers.

Schuh, J. H. (1988). Residence halls. In A. L. Rentz & G. L. Saddlemire (Eds.), *Student affairs functions in higher education* (pp. 227-260). Springfield, IL: Charles C. Thomas.

Schuh, J. H. & Shipton, W. C. (1983). Abuses encountered by resident assistants during an academic year. *Journal of College Student Personnel, 25*(5), 428-432.

Sedlacek, W. (1987). Black students on white campuses: 20 years of research. *Journal of College Student Personnel, 28*(6), 484-495.

Sherrill, J. M. (1989). Conclusions and additional sources of information. In J. M. Sherrill & D. G. Siegel (Eds.), *Responding to violence on campus* (New Directions for Student Services No. 47, pp. 89-97). San Francisco: Jossey-Bass Publishers.

Sherrill, J. M., & Siegel, D. G. (Eds.). (1989). *Responding to violence on campus* (New Directions for Student Services No. 47). San Francisco: Jossey-Bass Publishers.

Smith, M. C. (1989a) The ancestry of campus violence. In J. M. Sherrill & D. G. Siegel (Eds.), *Responding to violence on campus* (New Directions for Student Services No. 47, pp. 5-15). San Francisco: Jossey-Bass Publishers.

Smith, M. C. (1989b). *Crime and campus police: A handbook for police officers and administrators.* Asheville, NC: College Administration Publications, Inc.

Smith, M. C. (1990). Defensible space in campus design: One method for crime reduction in residence halls. *Journal of College and University Student Housing, 20*(1), 21-22.

Synfax Bulletin.

Synfax Weekly Report.

Synthesis: Law and Policy in Higher Education.

Taylor, C. (1986). Black students on predominantly white college campuses in the 1980s. *Journal of College Student Personnel, 27*(3), 196-208.

United States Department of Education. (1990). *The fund for the improvement of postsecondary education: Comprehensive program information and application procedures, fiscal year 1991.* Washington, DC: Author.

United States Department of Justice, Federal Bureau of Investigation. (1987). *Uniform Crime Report.* Washington, DC: U.S. Government Printing Office.

Appendix A

Cover Letter

[date]

[fullname]
[title]
[school]
[address]
[city], [state] [zip]

Dear [name]:

The residence hall system at your institution has been selected for participation in a study sponsored by the Research and Educational Foundation of the Association of College and University Housing Officers-International (ACUHO-I). Institutions were systematically selected from the *ACUHO-I 1991 Membership Directory* in such a way that the relatively small sample for this study would most accurately represent the total population of ACUHO-I member institutions in the United States according to state, region, district, size (based on numbers of students housed in residence halls), public vs. private status, and two-year vs. four-year status.

The formal title of the project, "Violence, Vandalism, and Verbal Harassment: A Study of Victimization in Residence Halls," describes a topic of growing concern to many housing professionals throughout the country. I believe that we face a great challenge in helping increasingly diverse populations of college students learn to live together with civility and respect for individual differences. Unfortunately, some students have reacted in negative ways to the increasing numbers or visibility of students identified as minorities according to their race/ethnicity, religion, or sexual preference.

Some housing officers report that racial, anti-Semitic, and homophobic incidents; incidents of acquaintance rape and courtship violence; and incidents in which Resident Assistants are harassed or otherwise "victimized" have grown in both number and severity during recent years. This study is designed to assess the nature and extent of this problem, factors that may be related to the problem, and means by which housing officers believe we can most effectively address the problem. The ultimate goal of the study is to help housing officers identify and understand problems of victimization in residence halls; develop programs, policies, and other measures to prevent or minimize the occurrence of such problems; and effectively deal with problems in the event that they do occur.

It should be emphasized from the outset that your participation in this study is voluntary. Your consent to participate will be indicated by your completion and return of the enclosed survey form. I assume full responsibility for maintaining the confidentiality of all responses. Your institution has been assigned a number, which will appear in the data set with institutional characteristics (for example, public/private, 2-year/4-year, ACUHO-I region) as identified in the ACUHO-I directory, but *without* the institution's name. All data will be reported at the aggregate level for the total sample and sub-samples (for example, small vs. medium vs. large housing systems). Answers to open-ended questions will be coded. In the event that I wish to make use of an example of a specific incident, a direct quotation, or any other response that could conceivably identify a specific institution or individual, I will contact the respondent and obtain a signed consent form before using such information.

I would be most grateful for your contributions to what I believe is an important study in the sense that it addresses a topic of great concern and has the potential to provide information and insights to help housing officers and their residence hall students.

Sincerely,

Carolyn J. Palmer, Ph.D.
Assistant Professor

Enclosures

Appendix B

Survey

VIOLENCE, VANDALISM, AND VERBAL HARASSMENT: A STUDY OF VICTIMIZATION IN RESIDENCE HALLS

Please take a moment to review the definitions of the following terms as they are used in this survey:

DURING THE LAST TWO YEARS is used as the time referent for many items. For example, you will be asked how often a certain type of incident has occurred "during the last two years." Please interpret this as two years (the 1989-90 and 1990-91 academic years) *plus* the time your school has been in session this fall.

VIOLENCE refers to any physical contact of a violent, angry, negative, uninvited, or unwanted nature with a *person*. Given this definition, even pushing, shoving, grabbing, or physically restraining someone against his or her will would be considered "violence"—even though no physical injury or serious harm is done.

VANDALISM refers to damage to or destruction of *property*. Graffiti in elevators, on walls, etc. would be included. For the purposes of this study, please interpret the term "violence" (defined above) as being perpetrated toward *human beings* and "vandalism" as being perpetrated toward *property*.

VERBAL HARASSMENT involves the use of spoken or written *language*. It may take many different forms, including (but not limited to) racist epithets or other comments, notes or letters, phone calls, etc. that are obscene, threatening, intimidating, insulting, etc. What distinguishes harassment from violence and vandalism (as these terms are to be interpreted in this study) is that it remains at the *verbal* (oral or written) level, but does not damage property. (For example, an obscene note or phone call would be considered "harassment," whereas the same obscenities spray painted on a wall would fall into the "graffiti" category and be considered "vandalism."

VICTIMS are categorized in five groups, examined on five different pages of this survey. These include students who are (1) resident assistants, (2) racial/ethnic minorities, (3) women, (4) gay or lesbian, and (5) Jewish. Please note on the reverse side of this page any special features of your student population that you feel may be relevant to this study. For example, if yours is an historically black institution or a religious-affiliated institution and white students or students not of the majority religion are victimized on the basis of their "minority" status, please note that.

In this study, your institution will be identified as School #[number]. Please review and, if necessary, correct the following information about your school:

                Size Category: [size] students housed in residence halls
                        State: [state]
             ACUHO-I Region: [region]
            ACUHO-I District: [district]
         Public/Private Status: [pupr]
       2-year/4-year Status: [years]

INFORMATION CONCERNING YOUR CAMPUS AND RESIDENCE HALL SYSTEM

A. The following questions concern numbers or percentages of students and staff. **If you do not know the exact figures, please give estimates.**

1. How many undergraduate students are enrolled on your campus? .... ____

2. How many graduate/professional students are enrolled on your campus? .... ____

3. How many undergraduates live in your residence halls? .... ____

4. How many graduate/professional students live in your residence halls? .... ____

5. Of the total number of students living in your residence halls, please list the number of:
   Men .... ____   International Students .... ____
   Women .... ____   American Students .... ____

6. Of the American students who live in residence halls, approximately how many would you estimate identify with each of the following racial/ethnic groups?
   White (non-Hispanic) .... ____   Native American Indian .... ____
   Hispanic/Latino .... ____   Alaskan Native .... ____
   Black/African-American .... ____   Hawaiian/Pacific Islander .... ____
   Asian-American .... ____   Other Racial/Ethnic Identity ____

7. How many Resident Assistants (RAs) work in your residence hall system? .... ____

8. Approximately how many of your RAs would you estimate identify with each of the following racial/ethnic groups?
   White (non-Hispanic) .... ____   Native American Indian .... ____
   Hispanic/Latino .... ____   Alaskan Native .... ____
   Black/African-American .... ____   Hawaiian/Pacific Islander .... ____
   Asian-American .... ____   Other Racial/Ethnic Identity ____

9. How many Hall Directors (professional live-in staff) do you employ? .... ____

10. How many of your Hall Directors would you estimate identify with each of the following racial/ethnic groups?
    White (non-Hispanic) .... ____   Native American Indian .... ____
    Hispanic/Latino .... ____   Alaskan Native .... ____
    Black/African-American .... ____   Hawaiian/Pacific Islander .... ____
    Asian-American .... ____   Other Racial/Ethnic Identity ____

Note: Responses to the next two items are acknowledged as "unknowns." Leave them blank if you wish. However, if you are willing to offer an "educated guess," it will be helpful in identifying approximate percentages estimated to identify with the groups in question.

11. Approximately what percentage of
    your residents are Jewish? .... ____%
    Approximately what percentage of
    your RAs are Jewish? .... ____%
    Approximately what percentage of
    your Hall Directors are Jewish? .... ____%
12. Approximately what percentage of
    your residents are gay/lesbian? .... ____%
    Approximately what percentage of
    your RAs are gay/lesbian? .... ____%
    Approximately what percentage of
    your Hall Directors are gay/lesbian? .... ____%

B. Please respond to each of the following by circling a number on the scale provided:

	Strongly Disagree						Strongly Agree

1. My institution is strongly committed to:

Admitting only the highest qualified students...............	1	2	3	4	5	6	7
Maximizing the quality of student life outside the classroom...............	1	2	3	4	5	6	7
Providing excellence in undergraduate education...............	1	2	3	4	5	6	7
Providing excellence in graduate/professional programs...............	1	2	3	4	5	6	7
Creating a multicultural campus community...............	1	2	3	4	5	6	7
Conducting research...............	1	2	3	4	5	6	7
Meeting the needs of diverse groups of students...............	1	2	3	4	5	6	7
Maintaining or enhancing its public image or prestige...............	1	2	3	4	5	6	7
Providing public service...............	1	2	3	4	5	6	7
Practicing affirmative action in employment...............	1	2	3	4	5	6	7
Practicing affirmative action in student admissions...............	1	2	3	4	5	6	7
Eliminating bigotry from the campus environment...............	1	2	3	4	5	6	7

2. Resident assistants (RAs) in our system are:

Exposed to a lot of information regarding issues of diversity in their staff development/training programs.....	1	2	3	4	5	6	7
Sensitive to issues affecting minority students...............	1	2	3	4	5	6	7
Responsive to the needs and problems of diverse groups...............	1	2	3	4	5	6	7

	Strongly Disagree						Strongly Agree

3. Professional staff in residence life (e.g., hall directors) are:

Exposed to a lot of information regarding issues of diversity in their staff development/training programs..... 1 2 3 4 5 6 7

Sensitive to issues affecting minority students....................... 1 2 3 4 5 6 7

Responsive to the needs and problems of diverse groups...................... 1 2 3 4 5 6 7

4. Residence hall programs focusing on diversity issues are:

Provided frequently..................................... 1 2 3 4 5 6 7
Usually attended by many students......... 1 2 3 4 5 6 7

5. Many of the students on this campus:

Have racist attitudes................................... 1 2 3 4 5 6 7
Engage in racist behaviors......................... 1 2 3 4 5 6 7
Have homophobic (anti-gay/lesbian) attitudes 1 2 3 4 5 6 7
Engage in homophobic behaviors.............. 1 2 3 4 5 6 7
Have anti-Semitic (anti-Jewish) attitudes............................... 1 2 3 4 5 6 7
Engage in anti-Semitic behaviors............... 1 2 3 4 5 6 7
Have sexist attitudes 1 2 3 4 5 6 7
Engage in sexist behaviors 1 2 3 4 5 6 7

6. There is a lot of racial tension on our campus................... 1 2 3 4 5 6 7

There is more racial tension than there was 5 years ago...................... 1 2 3 4 5 6 7

7. There is a lot of date rape and other violence toward women 1 2 3 4 5 6 7

There is more violence towards women than 5 years ago........................ 1 2 3 4 5 6 7

8. Does your school have a sexual harassment policy in effect for faculty/staff?... ____

9. Does your school have a racial harassment policy in effect for faculty/staff?... ____

10. Does your school have a policy concerning racial, sexual, or any other forms of harassment or "hate speech" in effect for *students*? .... ____

Survey

Victim Group #1: RESIDENT ASSISTANTS (RAs)

Violence

1. In your professional judgment (*whether or not the incidents were officially reported*), how many incidents in your residence halls during the past two years have involved violence towards RAs? .... ____
2. How many of these incidents were actually reported? .... ____
3. In how many of the reported incidents was the offender identified? .... ____
4. How many of the offender-identified incidents led to a disciplinary hearing? .... ____
5. How many of these disciplinary hearings led to disciplinary actions or sanctions? .... ____
6. How many of the disciplinary cases resulted in sanctions that you believe were sufficient to deter the offender from repeating similar behavior in the future? .... ____

Vandalism

1. In your professional judgment (*whether or not the incidents were officially reported*), how many incidents in your residence halls during the past two years have victimized RAs by some form of vandalism? .... ____
2. How many of these incidents were actually reported? .... ____
3. In how many of the reported incidents was the offender identified? .... ____
4. How many of the offender-identified incidents led to a disciplinary hearing? .... ____
5. How many of these disciplinary hearings led to disciplinary actions or sanctions? .... ____
6. How many of the disciplinary cases resulted in sanctions that you believe were sufficient to deter the offender from repeating similar behavior in the future? .... ____

Verbal Harassment

1. In your professional judgment (*whether or not the incidents were officially reported*), how many incidents in your residence halls during the past two years have victimized RAs by some form of verbal harassment? .... ____
2. How many of these incidents were actually reported? .... ____
3. In how many of the reported incidents was the offender identified? .... ____
4. How many of the offender-identified incidents led to a disciplinary hearing? .... ____
5. How many of these disciplinary hearings led to disciplinary actions or sanctions? .... ____
6. How many of the disciplinary cases resulted in sanctions that you believe were sufficient to deter the offender from repeating similar behavior in the future? .... ____

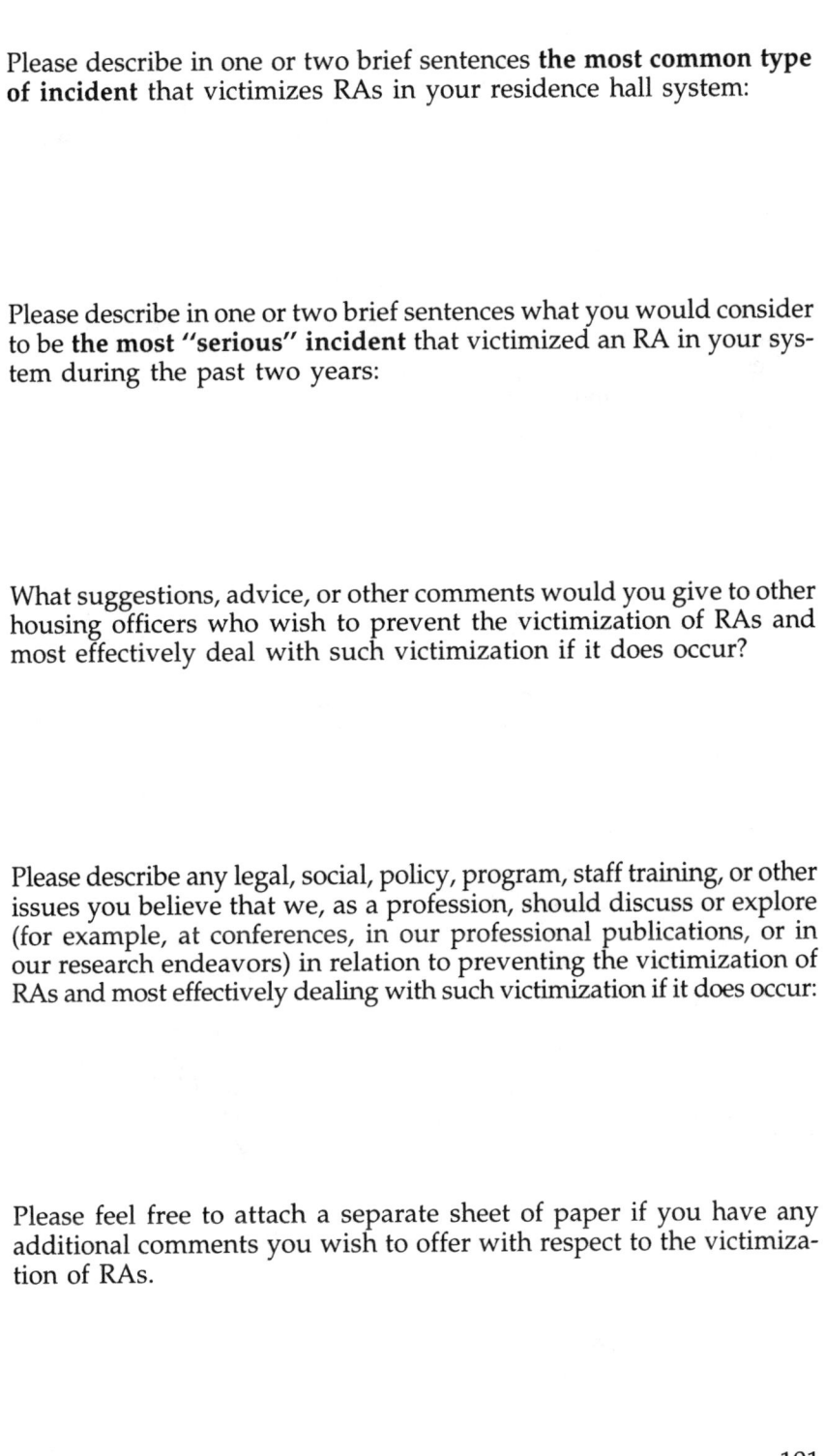

Please describe in one or two brief sentences **the most common type of incident** that victimizes RAs in your residence hall system:

Please describe in one or two brief sentences what you would consider to be **the most "serious" incident** that victimized an RA in your system during the past two years:

What suggestions, advice, or other comments would you give to other housing officers who wish to prevent the victimization of RAs and most effectively deal with such victimization if it does occur?

Please describe any legal, social, policy, program, staff training, or other issues you believe that we, as a profession, should discuss or explore (for example, at conferences, in our professional publications, or in our research endeavors) in relation to preventing the victimization of RAs and most effectively dealing with such victimization if it does occur:

Please feel free to attach a separate sheet of paper if you have any additional comments you wish to offer with respect to the victimization of RAs.

Victim Group #2: RACIAL/ETHNIC MINORITY STUDENTS

Violence

1. In your professional judgment (*whether or not the incidents were officially reported*), how many incidents in your residence halls during the past two years have involved violence towards racial/ethnic minority students? .... ____
2. How many of these incidents were actually reported? .... ____
3. In how many of the reported incidents was the offender identified? .... ____
4. How many of the offender-identified incidents led to a disciplinary hearing? .... ____
5. How many of these disciplinary hearings led to disciplinary actions or sanctions? .... ____
6. How many of the disciplinary cases resulted in sanctions that you believe were sufficient to deter the offender from repeating similar behavior in the future? .... ____

Vandalism

1. In your professional judgment (*whether or not the incidents were officially reported*), how many incidents in your residence halls during the past two years have victimized racial/ethnic minority students by some form of vandalism? .... ____
2. How many of these incidents were actually reported? .... ____
3. In how many of the reported incidents was the offender identified? .... ____
4. How many of the offender-identified incidents led to a disciplinary hearing? .... ____
5. How many of these disciplinary hearings led to disciplinary actions or sanctions? .... ____
6. How many of the disciplinary cases resulted in sanctions that you believe were sufficient to deter the offender from repeating similar behavior in the future? .... ____

Verbal Harassment

1. In your professional judgment (*whether or not the incidents were officially reported*), how many incidents in your residence halls during the past two years have victimized racial/ethnic minority students by some form of verbal harassment? .... ____
2. How many of these incidents were actually reported? .... ____
3. In how many of the reported incidents was the offender identified? .... ____
4. How many of the offender-identified incidents led to a disciplinary hearing? .... ____
5. How many of these disciplinary hearings led to disciplinary actions or sanctions? .... ____
6. How many of the disciplinary cases resulted in sanctions that you believe were sufficient to deter the offender from repeating similar behavior in the future? .... ____

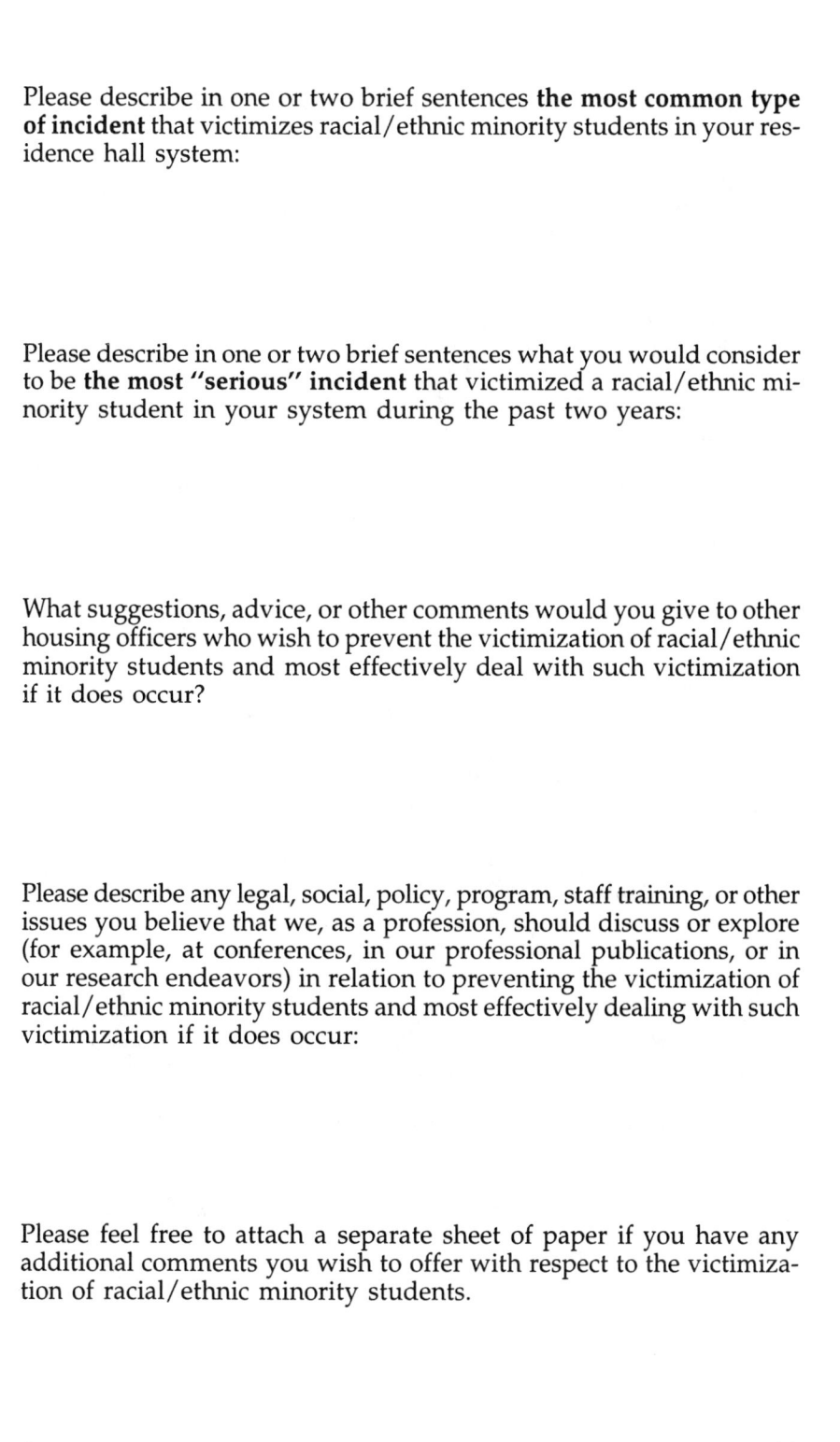

Please describe in one or two brief sentences **the most common type of incident** that victimizes racial/ethnic minority students in your residence hall system:

Please describe in one or two brief sentences what you would consider to be **the most "serious" incident** that victimized a racial/ethnic minority student in your system during the past two years:

What suggestions, advice, or other comments would you give to other housing officers who wish to prevent the victimization of racial/ethnic minority students and most effectively deal with such victimization if it does occur?

Please describe any legal, social, policy, program, staff training, or other issues you believe that we, as a profession, should discuss or explore (for example, at conferences, in our professional publications, or in our research endeavors) in relation to preventing the victimization of racial/ethnic minority students and most effectively dealing with such victimization if it does occur:

Please feel free to attach a separate sheet of paper if you have any additional comments you wish to offer with respect to the victimization of racial/ethnic minority students.

Victim Group #3: WOMEN STUDENTS

Violence
1. In your professional judgment (*whether or not the incidents were officially reported*), how many incidents in your residence halls during the past two years have involved violence towards women students?...................... ____
2. How many of these incidents were actually reported? .... ____
3. In how many of the reported incidents was the offender identified?.. ____
4. How many of the offender-identified incidents led to a disciplinary hearing?... ____
5. How many of these disciplinary hearings led to disciplinary actions or sanctions?............................... ____
6. How many of the disciplinary cases resulted in sanctions that you believe were sufficient to deter the offender from repeating similar behavior in the future?...................... ____

Vandalism
1. In your professional judgment (*whether or not the incidents were officially reported*), how many incidents in your residence halls during the past two years have victimized women students by some form of vandalism? .... ____
2. How many of these incidents were actually reported? .... ____
3. In how many of the reported incidents was the offender identified?.. ____
4. How many of the offender-identified incidents led to a disciplinary hearing?... ____
5. How many of these disciplinary hearings led to disciplinary actions or sanctions?............................... ____
6. How many of the disciplinary cases resulted in sanctions that you believe were sufficient to deter the offender from repeating similar behavior in the future?...................... ____

Verbal Harassment
1. In your professional judgment (*whether or not the incidents were officially reported*), how many incidents in your residence halls during the past two years have victimized women students by some form of verbal harassment? ...... ____
2. How many of these incidents were actually reported? .... ____
3. In how many of the reported incidents was the offender identified?.. ____
4. How many of the offender-identified incidents led to a disciplinary hearing?... ____
5. How many of these disciplinary hearings led to disciplinary actions or sanctions?............................... ____
6. How many of the disciplinary cases resulted in sanctions that you believe were sufficient to deter the offender from repeating similar behavior in the future?...................... ____

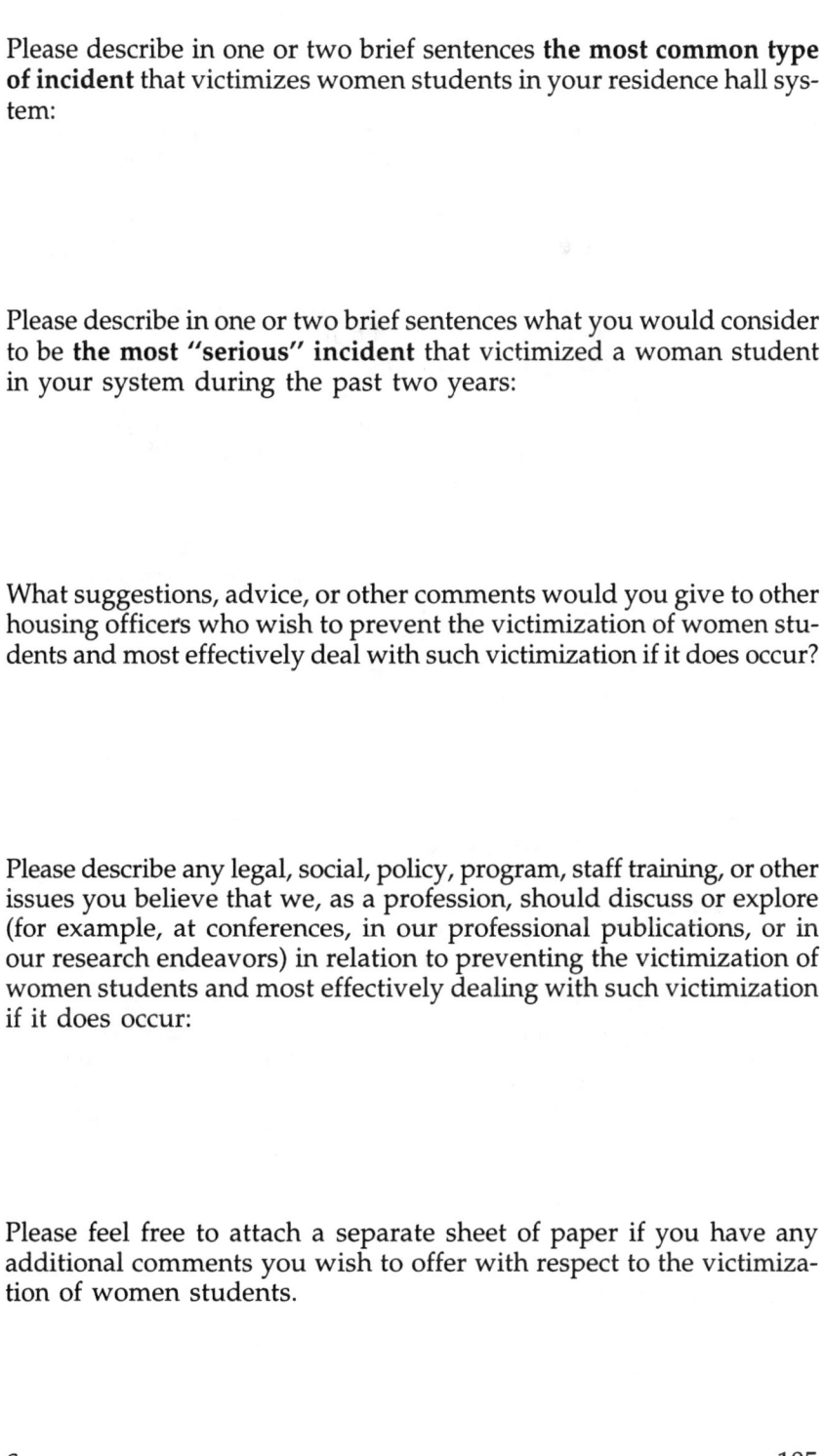

Please describe in one or two brief sentences **the most common type of incident** that victimizes women students in your residence hall system:

Please describe in one or two brief sentences what you would consider to be **the most "serious" incident** that victimized a woman student in your system during the past two years:

What suggestions, advice, or other comments would you give to other housing officers who wish to prevent the victimization of women students and most effectively deal with such victimization if it does occur?

Please describe any legal, social, policy, program, staff training, or other issues you believe that we, as a profession, should discuss or explore (for example, at conferences, in our professional publications, or in our research endeavors) in relation to preventing the victimization of women students and most effectively dealing with such victimization if it does occur:

Please feel free to attach a separate sheet of paper if you have any additional comments you wish to offer with respect to the victimization of women students.

Victim Group #4: GAY/LESBIAN STUDENTS

Violence
1. In your professional judgment (*whether or not the incidents were officially reported*), how many incidents in your residence halls during the past two years have involved violence towards gay/lesbian students? .... ____
2. How many of these incidents were actually reported? .... ____
3. In how many of the reported incidents was the offender identified? .... ____
4. How many of the offender-identified incidents led to a disciplinary hearing? .... ____
5. How many of these disciplinary hearings led to disciplinary actions or sanctions? .... ____
6. How many of the disciplinary cases resulted in sanctions that you believe were sufficient to deter the offender from repeating similar behavior in the future? .... ____

Vandalism
1. In your professional judgment (*whether or not the incidents were officially reported*), how many incidents in your residence halls during the past two years have victimized gay/lesbian students by some form of vandalism? .... ____
2. How many of these incidents were actually reported? .... ____
3. In how many of the reported incidents was the offender identified? .... ____
4. How many of the offender-identified incidents led to a disciplinary hearing? .... ____
5. How many of these disciplinary hearings led to disciplinary actions or sanctions? .... ____
6. How many of the disciplinary cases resulted in sanctions that you believe were sufficient to deter the offender from repeating similar behavior in the future? .... ____

Verbal Harassment
1. In your professional judgment (*whether or not the incidents were officially reported*), how many incidents in your residence halls during the past two years have victimized gay/lesbian students by some form of verbal harassment? .... ____
2. How many of these incidents were actually reported? .... ____
3. In how many of the reported incidents was the offender identified? .... ____
4. How many of the offender-identified incidents led to a disciplinary hearing? .... ____
5. How many of these disciplinary hearings led to disciplinary actions or sanctions? .... ____
6. How many of the disciplinary cases resulted in sanctions that you believe were sufficient to deter the offender from repeating similar behavior in the future? .... ____

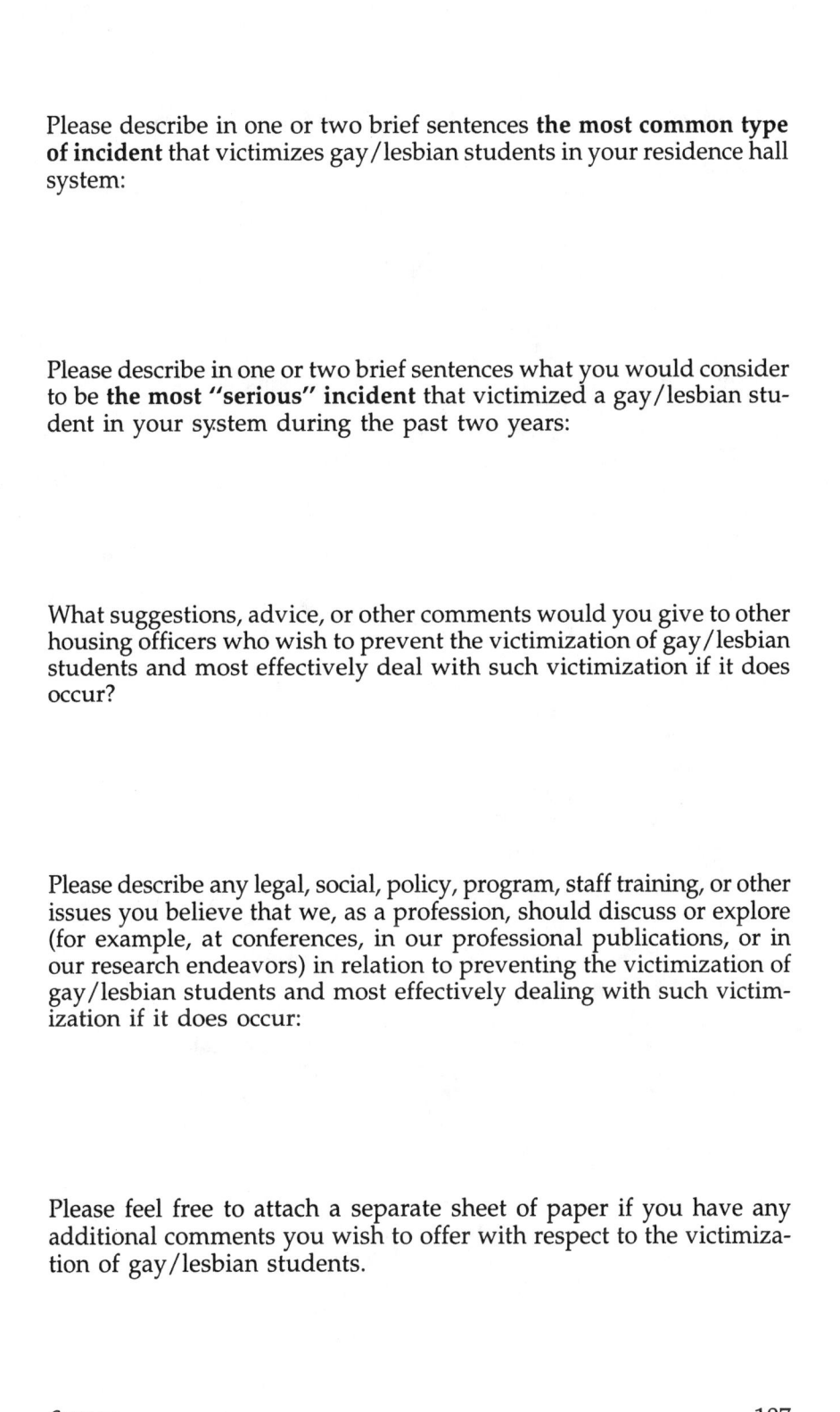

Please describe in one or two brief sentences **the most common type of incident** that victimizes gay/lesbian students in your residence hall system:

Please describe in one or two brief sentences what you would consider to be **the most "serious" incident** that victimized a gay/lesbian student in your system during the past two years:

What suggestions, advice, or other comments would you give to other housing officers who wish to prevent the victimization of gay/lesbian students and most effectively deal with such victimization if it does occur?

Please describe any legal, social, policy, program, staff training, or other issues you believe that we, as a profession, should discuss or explore (for example, at conferences, in our professional publications, or in our research endeavors) in relation to preventing the victimization of gay/lesbian students and most effectively dealing with such victimization if it does occur:

Please feel free to attach a separate sheet of paper if you have any additional comments you wish to offer with respect to the victimization of gay/lesbian students.

Victim Group #5: JEWISH STUDENTS

Violence

1. In your professional judgment (*whether or not the incidents were officially reported*), how many incidents in your residence halls during the past two years have involved violence towards Jewish students?........................ ____
2. How many of these incidents were actually reported? .... ____
3. In how many of the reported incidents was the offender identified?.. ____
4. How many of the offender-identified incidents led to a disciplinary hearing?... ____
5. How many of these disciplinary hearings led to disciplinary actions or sanctions?............................. ____
6. How many of the disciplinary cases resulted in sanctions that you believe were sufficient to deter the offender from repeating similar behavior in the future?.................... ____

Vandalism

1. In your professional judgment (*whether or not the incidents were officially reported*), how many incidents in your residence halls during the past two years have victimized Jewish students by some form of vandalism?...................... ____
2. How many of these incidents were actually reported? .... ____
3. In how many of the reported incidents was the offender identified?.. ____
4. How many of the offender-identified incidents led to a disciplinary hearing?... ____
5. How many of these disciplinary hearings led to disciplinary actions or sanctions?............................. ____
6. How many of the disciplinary cases resulted in sanctions that you believe were sufficient to deter the offender from repeating similar behavior in the future?.................... ____

Verbal Harassment

1. In your professional judgment (*whether or not the incidents were officially reported*), how many incidents in your residence halls during the past two years have victimized Jewish students by some form of verbal harassment?........ ____
2. How many of these incidents were actually reported? .... ____
3. In how many of the reported incidents was the offender identified?.. ____
4. How many of the offender-identified incidents led to a disciplinary hearing?... ____
5. How many of these disciplinary hearings led to disciplinary actions or sanctions?............................. ____
6. How many of the disciplinary cases resulted in sanctions that you believe were sufficient to deter the offender from repeating similar behavior in the future?.................... ____

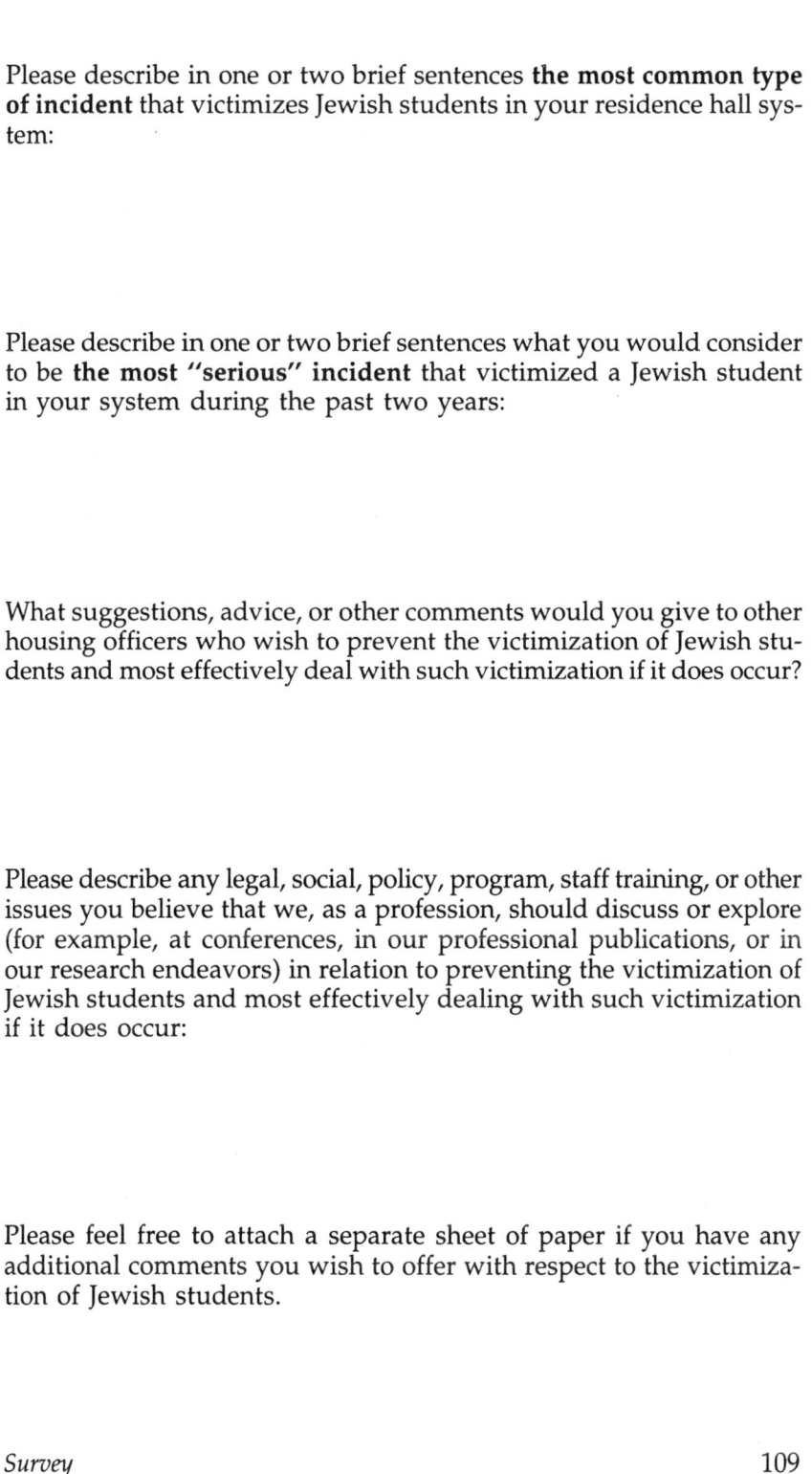

Please describe in one or two brief sentences **the most common type of incident** that victimizes Jewish students in your residence hall system:

Please describe in one or two brief sentences what you would consider to be **the most "serious" incident** that victimized a Jewish student in your system during the past two years:

What suggestions, advice, or other comments would you give to other housing officers who wish to prevent the victimization of Jewish students and most effectively deal with such victimization if it does occur?

Please describe any legal, social, policy, program, staff training, or other issues you believe that we, as a profession, should discuss or explore (for example, at conferences, in our professional publications, or in our research endeavors) in relation to preventing the victimization of Jewish students and most effectively dealing with such victimization if it does occur:

Please feel free to attach a separate sheet of paper if you have any additional comments you wish to offer with respect to the victimization of Jewish students.